"One of the appealing qualities of watercolour is its transparency, which makes it the ideal medium for capturing the subtleties of different light effects in nature, and gives a wonderful luminosity to the subject. In its topographical form with its prerequisite precise drawing it blends fine architecture with its complimentary landscape. This can clearly be seen in Turner's early work."

Professor Ken Howard O.B.E., R.A., R.W.S.

To Sheila

First published in Great Britain in 2012 by

CONTEMPORARY WATERCOLOURS
57 Windmill Street
Gravesend
Kent DA12 1BB
Tel: 01474 535922
Website: www.contemporarywatercolours.co.uk

Set in Times New Roman.   Artwork by Janet Davie.   Project co-ordinator: Sue Burgess

Printed by Oriental Press Limited, UAE
Reprographics by Printcom.co.uk Ltd

ISBN 978 - 0 - 9526480 - 4 - 8

Front cover: **Eton College** - *John Doyle*
Back Cover: **St. Peter's School, York** - *Ken Howard;* **Monmouth College** - *Clifford Bayly*
Portora Royal School, Enniskillen - *Grahame Booth;* **Fettes College, Edinburgh** - *James Porteous Wood*

PORTRAITS OF BRITISH SCHOOLS

by
Distinguished British Artists

**Clifford Bayly   Grahame Booth   Jane Carpanini   John Doyle   Dennis Flanders
Ken Howard   Ken Messer   John Newberry   James Porteous Wood
Hubert Pragnell   Dennis Roxby Bott   Denis Ryan**

Text by
MALCOLM HORTON

CONTEMPORARY WATERCOLOURS

CONTENTS

CONTENTS

76

GEOGRAPHICAL INDEX OF SCHOOLS

Foreword

International comparisons rate Britain's independent schools as among the very best in the world. What this volume of watercolours illustrates is that often their architecture and settings are also remarkable.

The public schools were so called because they were not private institutions but charitable foundations available to scholarship boys and fee-payers. The history of education in our country is the story of the ancient schools, the grammar schools and the Victorian boarding-schools, and all are well-represented here.

The earliest schools, founded by great men and monarchs to educate the servants of church and state, have at their heart buildings with all the patina of age and continuity. Plain living and high thinking for more than six centuries gives an extraordinary atmosphere to College Hall at Winchester, and School Yard at Eton is bounded by the oldest brick building in England still in continual use. King's Canterbury and Westminster lie at the very heart of the country's great institutions and use an Abbey and a Cathedral as their school chapels. Pupils at the one are at the very centre of English Christianity; at the other they can tell the time from Big Ben and attend debates in the mother of parliaments. Their location reminds us of the central part education has played throughout the centuries.

Manchester Grammar School and Bolton School are typical of the schools founded in the sixteenth century – sometimes by royal permission , sometimes by local worthies - to supplement or replace the monastic and church schools abolished at the Reformation. They emerged in later centuries as academic power-houses. By the second half of the nineteenth century some of the best early grammar-schools had outgrown their cramped inner-city premises and moved to more spacious sites. 'Dr Bruce's Academy' grew into Belfast Royal Academy. Shrewsbury took over a fine eighteenth-century workhouse and green fields on a bluff above the Severn. Charterhouse rebuilt itself handsomely near Godalming.

That period saw a dramatic growth in education. Forster's Education Act provided for compulsory education for all , for the first time, up to the age of twelve. Among the middle classes there was a huge new demand for boarding. For one thing the Empire needed more and more educated young men prepared to serve abroad, and, for another, increasingly-prosperous parents began to see merit in a broader concept of all-round education than was offered in the local school. Radley and Malvern, Marlborough, St Edward's Oxford and Wycombe Abbey, fine schools set among spacious playing-fields, were typical of the time. Architecturally the most exuberant was Fettes, which is easily mistaken for one of the chateaux of the Loire.

Sadly - but, given the constraints of cost, I suppose inevitably- even the most beautiful ancient schools have later additional buildings of which they cannot always be proud. This collection of watercolours, however, concentrates on what is good. From the beauty of the early collegiate foundations which rival Oxford and Cambridge colleges through to the confident dignity of early twentieth-century public buildings, here is the full range of school architecture at its best.

Sir Eric Anderson
Former Head Master and Provost of Eton

Introduction

The schools featured in this book contain some of the most splendid architecture and scenery in The British Isles.

The medium used to portray all but one of the sixty five schools is the quintessentially British genre of watercolour painting which is ideal for the portrayal of architectural subjects.

The high period of British watercolour painting was the hundred or so years after the mid-18th century. The work of Turner, Constable, De Wint, Palmer, Girtin, Cotman and Sandby popularised the watercolour art form and led, in 1804, to the foundation of the Royal Watercolour Society; the oldest organisation of its kind in the world.

This great tradition is carried on by the present 90 members and none more so than those eight who have contributed to the illustrations in this book.

I am not an expert on watercolour technique, so I have generally let the paintings speak for themselves with just a title for scenes depicted and the artist's attribution. I am not a historian either, but I could not resist the temptation to add some historical notes and unique anecdotes associated with the schools. Like our great universities, the whole of British history seems to have marched through, or been influenced, by the pupils of our leading schools. Wherever possible, I have had the factual accuracy checked by Heads and Archivists at the schools concerned.

The genesis for most of this collection of watercolours are the series of paintings commissioned, by my company Contemporary Watercolours, from which limited edition prints have been made, for dissemination to the former pupils of the schools concerned. These have been produced over a period of 25 years and encompass the whole of the British Isles including all but six of the forty traditional counties of England.

I have been privileged to work with some of the most talented artists in the land and to have received the unfailing support and advice from the Heads and staff of the schools featured. I must give special thanks to Janet Davie, our designer from the outset in 1987, who was responsible for the beautifully hand painted coats of arms which surround the contents pages. Without all of these concomitant contributions this book would not have been possible. I thank them all.

Malcolm Horton
Tutt Hill, Kent

The Royal Watercolour Society

The Royal Watercolour Society (R.W.S.) was founded in 1804 and received its Royal Patronage in 1884. In February 2004, it celebrated its bicentenary with a visit from H.M. Queen Elizabeth II and is the oldest society of its kind in the world. Society Members have included Peter de Wint, David Cox, Helen Allingham, John Sell Cotman, Samuel Palmer, Sir Edward Burne Jones, John Singer Sargeant, Arthur Rackman, Sir William Russell Flint and Charles Knight.

The Society is now based at the Bankside Gallery which is situated on the South Bank of the River Thames overlooking St Paul's Cathedral. It was opened on 11th November 1980 by Her Majesty the Queen. The area is of great historical importance, and is now the focus for the best contemporary art with the opening of the new Tate Gallery of Modern Art. There are some 90 members of the R.W.S., both Fellows and Associates and admission to the Society is determined by annual election.

The majority of paintings in this book have been contributed by R.W.S. members and, of course, they are indicated by the designation 'R.W.S.'

Clifford Bayly, R.W.S.

Clifford was trained at St. Martin's and Camberwell Schools of Art and was elected a Fellow of the Royal Watercolour Society in 1984. He was, for twenty years, Head of Graphic Design Degree Courses at Maidstone College of Art. He has exhibited regularly at the Royal Academy Summer Exhibition and Bankside Gallery, home of the Royal Watercolour Society of which he was Vice President for three years. He has been a winner of the prestigious annual Singer Friedlander/Sunday Times National Watercolour competition. He now lives in Australia where he has had numerous solo exhibitions in the state capitals, and spends the summer months in Britain.

Grahame Booth, U.W.S.

Grahame is a past President of the Ulster Watercolour Society and a member of the Arts Society of Ulster. He paints exclusively in watercolour and as well as exhibiting widely, teaches watercolour at a number of workshops throughout Northern Ireland. He is a visiting tutor at Art Club and Art Centre workshops. Subject matter is unimportant as it is the atmosphere, light and colour in the subject that are the important factors and consequently his material includes industrial subjects and interiors as well as more traditional scenes. As a "loose realist" he aims to capture the essentials of a subject as purely and economically as possible. His work is represented in private and public collections including Belfast City Council and Ulster Independent Clinic. He was a finalist in the Channel 4 Watercolour Challenge and has won many awards including most recently the Castlereagh Council Tyrone Guthrie Bursary Award.

Jane Carpanini, R.W.S., R.W.A.

Jane was born in Bedfordshire and was first elected to the Royal Watercolour Society in 1978, establishing a reputation for expansively composed and meticulous watercolours. She was trained at Brighton College of Art and the University of Reading. Her work is in the collections of the National Library and National Museum of Wales. She is also a member of the Royal West of England Academy and the Royal Cambrian Academy, and exhibits with these societies. She has served as the Vice President and Honorary Treasurer of the Royal Watercolour Society. In 1983 she was the winner of the prestigious Hunting Group's Prize for the Watercolour of the Year by a British Artist.

John Doyle, M.B.E., P.P.R.W.S.

John was born in Dulwich, London and is a past President of the Royal Watercolour Society and has had many exhibitions in major galleries in London and Canterbury Cathedral. A book, entitled "An Artists Journey down the Thames" was published in 1989. He undertook a peripatetic journey retracing and painting in St. Augustine's footsteps from Rome to Canterbury to celebrate, in 1997, the fourteen hundredth anniversary of this famous event. The culmination of which was an exhibition at Canterbury Cathedral of the paintings made in the course of this journey. John now lives on the edge of Romney Marsh in Kent and readily acknowledges the help and encouragement he received in the early years from the distinguished painter John Ward.

Dennis Flanders, R.W.S., R.B.A.

Dennis was born in London and was unquestionably one of the greatest pencil and watercolour artists of the twentieth century. He attended evening classes in antique drawing at Regents Street Polytechnic whilst working for a firm of fashionable interior decorators. He painted the scenery and architecture of the British Isles for over sixty years before his death in 1994 and has been called the "Canaletto of our time" by Peterborough in the Daily Telegraph. He was for some years a graphic reporter with the 'Illustrated London News' and his pictures of London during the Blitz are treasures of the Guildhall Library and the Imperial War Museum. A Freeman of the City of London, he was a member of the Art Workers Guild and served as Master in 1975. Two previous books have been published containing the body of his lifetime's work, "Britannia" in 1984 and "Watercolours in Academe" in 1994.

Professor Ken Howard, O.B.E., R.A., R.W.S.

Ken was born in London and is a member of the Royal Academy and Royal Watercolour Society. He is also president of the New English Arts Club, that bastion of figurative painting and drawing. He was official war artist in Northern Ireland in 1973 and 1978. Since his National Service in the Royal Marines 1953–55 he has had a close association with the British Army, undertaking special commissions for them throughout the world, including portraits of the Royal Family. Ken's work is held in public collections including the Imperial War Museum, Ulster Museum, National Army Museum and the Guildhall Art Gallery. He has studios in London, Cornwall and Venice. Several books on his life and works have been published including "The paintings of Ken Howard" in 1992; "Ken Howard A Personal View" in 1998 and more recently, in 2011, "Light and Dark - The Autobiography of Ken Howard". He has regular exhibitions at the Richard Green Gallery in London.

Ken Messer.

Ken was born in Newport Monmouth and educated at the City of Oxford School. On leaving school he went into accountancy, leaving it after six years to fly all over the world with BOAC. A motor accident cut short his flying career and at the age of thirty-three he joined Pergamon Press in their design department, after six years he became Studio Manager, in charge of Art and Design. In 1974 he left publishing to freelance as a graphic designer and painting watercolours started to take up more of his time. He has since won prizes in three consecutive biennial Saunders "Artist in Watercolour" international competitions and in the Artist Magazine watercolour competition. Prints of his work have been published by Rosenstiels, Kingfisher Prints, Templecrest Art and the Burford Gallery. His work has hung in the Royal Institute of Painters in Watercolour annual exhibitions at the Mall Galleries

John Newberry, R.W.S.

John was born in Horsham, Sussex and was educated at Kingswood School, in Bath. He studied architecture at Cambridge and fine art at Newcastle. He taught at the Ruskin School of Drawing and Fine Art at Oxford from 1963-1989 and was Acting Head in the last two years. John now paints full time and specialises in buildings and landscapes with strong perspectives and unusual light effects. He exhibited for many years in Oxford but now shows regularly in London and Somerset.

James Porteous Wood, R.S.W.

James was born in Edinburgh and educated at George Heriot's School. He was trained at Edinburgh College of Art and in 1945 he became the youngest elected member of the Royal Scottish Watercolour Society. His murals and paintings are held in many of the world's premier collections including royal and Presidential Palaces in Africa and the Middle and Far East. For the past 50 years his work has regularly appeared in the National Press and for 25 years he was Artist and Designer in residence for Aspreys of Bond Street. After retiring in 1981, he became a full time artist based near his home, near Fort William, until his death in 2005.

Hubert Pragnell, M.A., A.T.D., N.D.D.

Hubert was born in London and he trained at Goldsmith's College, London, and the Ruskin School of Drawing and Fine Art, Oxford. He also has an M.A. in history from the University of Kent and has written and illustrated a number of books on architecture including 'Britain, a guide to Architectural Styles', 'Industrial Britain, an architectural history' and 'Oxford in Watercolour'. He retired from full time teaching after 36 years, mostly in the independent sector as Head of Art, and History of Art, and apart from part-time university teaching, spends much of his spare time painting.

Dennis Roxby Bott, R.W.S.

Dennis was born in Chingford, Essex, and attended the prestigious Norwich School of Art where he studied fine art painting and obtained a Dip.A.D. (Fine Art). He was elected a member of the Royal Watercolour Society in 1981. Dennis, who now lives in Sussex, has had regular one man exhibitions in London and Sussex notably Ebury Street Galleries, SW1, Worthing Art Gallery and Museum, Lannards Gallery, Billingshurst and the Ogle Galleries. He is a regular exhibitor at the annual spring and autumn Royal Watercolour exhibitions at the Bankside Gallery and in 1992 he was a prize winner at the annual Discerning Eye Exhibition at The Mall Gallery in London and in 2011, Dennis won the 'Smith & Williamson Cityscape Prize' in the Sunday Times Watercolour Competition. His commissions include the Wardroom of H.M. Royal Yacht Britannia, Sotheby's and the National Trust.

Denis Ryan, R.W.S.

Denis was born in London and studied for an M.A. in fine Art at Watford, Hornsey and Ravensbourne Colleges of Art from 1966 – 1972. In 2008 he was elected an Associate Member of the Royal Watercolour Society (A.R.W.S.) His career began in film animation and later illustration. He worked on award-winning films such as Watership Down and The Wall and has commissions for illustrations from most of the leading publishing houses. Having worked in commercial art since leaving art school he is now concentrating on pursuing his love of fine art, in particular painting with watercolour. As his website shows his peregrinations worldwide in search of subject matter result in paintings which are delightfully idiosyncratic.

Malcolm Horton, author and publisher.

Malcolm Horton was articled to a City of London firm of chartered accountants and qualified in 1966. He spent twenty years in industry and commerce with companies such as Beck and Politzer, Esso Petroleum and BOC International. The latter part of this period was spent in the printing industry, where he was, successively, chief executive of Williams Lea, and of international fine art printers, Westerham Press. In 1986 he set up an accountancy practice as well as a fine-art publishing business, Contemporary Watercolours. The watercolour business has not only allowed him to work with some of Britain's most talented watercolour painters, but his peregrinations have given him an intimate knowledge of the beautiful towns and cities of the British Isles. His previous books are "Watercolours in Academe", "Oxford Watercolours", "Cambridge Watercolours" and "Artists' Oxford". His hobbies include playing squash and watching Charlton Athletic F.C. He is married and lives with his wife, Sheila, on the Chart Hills, just outside Ashford in Kent.

BELFAST ROYAL ACADEMY

Grahame Booth

Crombie Building

The Belfast Royal Academy (commonly shortened to BRA) is the oldest school in the city of Belfast. It is also co-educational and non-denominational. At the time of its foundation in 1785, educational provision in Belfast was sadly lacking, with individual tuition being provided by a few ad hoc schools and educated gentlemen who were usually ministers of religion. Trinity College Dublin was the only university in Ireland and, since it was effectively an Anglican institution, Presbyterians preferred to go to Scotland for university training while Catholics went abroad, mainly to France and Spain (Catholics at this time were barred from Oxford & Cambridge).

It was against this background that a group of wealthy Belfast merchants and bankers decided to found an academy. Their number included the founders of the Belfast Bank: John Holmes, John Brown, John Hamilton and John Ewing, whose bank was known colloquially as the 'Bank of The Four Johns'. Another subscriber to the new academy was wealthy merchant, Waddel Cunningham and the Academy's accredited founder and first Headmaster, Dr James Crombie.

Originally situated near St Anne's Parish Church in what is now Academy Street, it moved to its present location in Cliftonville Road in 1880. For more than a century the School was named 'Belfast Academy' until in 1888 Queen Victoria granted permission for the School to style itself 'Belfast Royal Academy'.

The new school in Cliftonville Road had been designed by the Belfast Architects, Young & McKenzie, in the Gothic Scottish Baronial style popular in Edinburgh at the time. Local scrabe sandstone was the main building material used.

Early in the Academy's life, in 1792, there occurred an incident which has gone down in Belfast educational folklore as the 'barring out' incident. A group of ten schoolboys barricaded themselves in the mathematical classroom. A letter headed 'Liberty Hall' was sent by the students to their masters in which they stated their refusal to surrender until their demands had been met. They were armed with five pistols and a large quantity of gun powder and shot. After attempts to remove them by force failed, the Mayor of Belfast, the Revd Williams Bristowe was summoned to 'read the Riot Act' to the boys but he failed to end the barring out and one of the boys opened fire on him. The siege was finally ended and the boys were beaten and expelled.

Of the Academy's former pupils in the 19th century, perhaps the most colourful was Sir Henry Pottinger who, in 1843, played a major role in forcing the Chinese Empire to cede Hong Kong to Britain. He was known to the Chinese as 'the barbarian Pottinger' and became the first Governor of the new colony. Hong Kong was handed back to the Chinese in 1997.

BENENDEN SCHOOL

Jane Carpanini

The Terrace

In the early 1920s due to an unprecedented demand for more and better public schools for girls, Miss Frances Dove, the dynamic founder and headmistress of Wycombe Abbey School, challenged members of her staff to start another school like her own 1896 foundation. Three of her staff; Miss Bird, Miss Hindle and Miss Sheldon, took up her challenge.

In July 1923 a furnished school in Bickley, South London, was found and became the temporary home of the School until January 1924 when a permanent home was secured. Hempstead Park, a Victorian mansion set in 250 acres of Wealden countryside near the village of Benenden in Kent, was purchased from Lord Rothermere for £22,500. The School was named Benenden School to avoid confusion with Hemel Hempstead in Hertfordshire.

The Hempstead Park Estate is of great historical interest being mentioned in Domesday as belonging to Bishop Odo, half-brother of William the Conqueror. In 1388 Richard II granted Hempstead Park to William de Guldeford who immediately built a fine manor house on the estate. The Guldeford dynasty was to remain in occupation for over 300 years during which time, in 1573, Elizabeth I and her entourage stayed for three days.

In 1718, Sir Thomas Guldeford, with mounting debts and no heirs, sold Hempstead Park to Sir John Norris who was Admiral of the British Fleet. In 1857, a later owner, Gathorne Hardy, who became Earl of Cranbrook, demolished the Elizabethan house and built a new mansion to the designs of David Brandon. Finally, Sir Vere Harmsworth, later Lord Rothermere, purchased the estate in 1910; remodelled the house, divided it up and sold the house and immediate grounds to Benenden School in 1924.

The estate on which Benenden School resides is of great historical interest, but it is the general landscape in the heart of the Weald of Kent which is of special interest. The Weald of Kent was, until the late middle ages, the most densely forested region of England. The mighty oaks of the Weald were gradually thinned out when farmers from the Kentish uplands created clearings in order to feed their beasts on the abundant supply of acorns. These clearings were known as 'dens' hence the name Benenden. There are over 30 place names in Kent ending in the suffix 'den'.

Another contributory factor causing the mighty oaks of the Weald to be cleared was the emergence of the native English iron smelting industry fuelled by charcoal from the abundant oak trees and local iron ore deposits. The iron industry in Kent reached its peak in the late 16th century. In the 17th century the industry moved to the coal producing areas of South Wales and the North of England. Timber for shipbuilding particularly during the Tudor period also denuded the oak forests.

The setting of Benenden School in the Weald of Kent and the history of Hempstead Park have no doubt made more than just a passing impact on its pupils. Distinguished alumni include The Princess Royal; the journalist Penny Junor; actress Rachel Weiss; Sue Ryder and Eliza Mannigham-Buller, former Director General of MI5.

BERKHAMSTED SCHOOL

Jane Carpanini

Chapel and Lychgate

The mid-16th century was a time of great religious turbulence. The Protestant revolution begun by Henry VIII and carried on even more zealously by his young son, Edward VI, was dramatically reversed in 1553 by the ascension to the throne of the Catholic Mary I. Much bloodshed ensued. Then in 1558 Elizabeth I came to the throne and it was wise to be a Protestant again.

Scholastic establishments were required to reflect the ever changing religious climate, and so, between 1555 – 1567, Berkhamsted School had three changes of headmaster. It was still only a fledgling foundation at this time, having been founded in 1541 during the reign of Henry VIII by Dr John Incent, former Dean of St Pauls. Its first building known as 'Old Hall' was completed before Dr Incent's death in 1546.

In 1567 William Saltmarsh was appointed Headmaster and the next 33 years under his rule were the most successful in the School's history. On Saltmarsh's death in 1600 Thomas Hunt became Headmaster for the next 36 years. A period of stability and growth even though Hunt managed to lose four wives in this time!

Not long after Hunt's death the School was plagued not only by the disease (two headmasters died in 1643 and 1648 from the epidemic) but also by the English Civil War 1642 – 1651. Berkhamsted was in the eye of the storm, being on one of the main routes from London to Oxford where Charles I had made his wartime headquarters. As a result pupil numbers fell from 80 to around 10.

In 1668 matters were not helped when the notorious Thomas Fosson (a friend of Samuel Pepys) was appointed Headmaster. He famously declared publicly that he cared not whether he had any scholars as they were such a bother. His resignation followed shortly after.

Like most schools in 18th century England, Berkhamsted suffered from the general apathy affecting schools at this time (by 1746 numbers had reduced to five). The decadence and corruption in Church and State nationally were partly to blame together with the disappearance in the face of mammon of free education for the poor; a founding principal of most early Public Schools. Moreover the upper classes, in the face of this decline, preferred to have their children taught privately.

Fortunately, a new morality took hold in the 19th century with the emergence of the middle classes who demanded a reorientation of the Public Schools. It was in Victoria's time that the real flowering of the Public School ethos began. Many new schools were opened and old schools, including Berkhamsted, were revived.

17

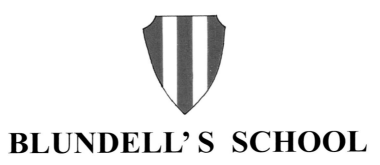

BLUNDELL'S SCHOOL

Denis Ryan

Tower and Chapel

In Elizabethan England Tiverton was a prosperous West Country town ranking with Plymouth and Exeter in importance. It owed its wealth to the cloth trade and one of its most successful merchants, Peter Blundell, although of humble origins, became one of the wealthiest men in Devon. When he died, in 1601, he left lands and money to found a school in his home town to maintain sound learning and true religion in the new Puritan/Protestant ethos. The Cambridge colleges of Emmanuel and Sidney Sussex had only recently been founded to espouse these same sentiments as an antidote to 'Popery'.

The Executor of Peter Blundell's Will was his friend, Sir John Popham, who was the Chief Justice of England and a most enthusiastic Puritan. His Crown prosecutions included Mary Queen of Scots and Guy Fawkes. He speedily carried out Blundell's wishes and, by 1604, had established a school in the centre of Tiverton on the banks of the River Lowman, a tributary of the Exe. No expense was spared, as Blundell's was to be a school much larger and grander than any other in the West Country. Additionally money was given to provide scholarships at Balliol College, Oxford and Sidney Sussex College, Cambridge. Old Blundellians have been Masters of their College at Balliol (John Davey 1785-98) and Sidney Sussex (Knox Shaw 1945-57). To this day a representative of Balliol sits on the Board of Governors.

Blundell's is one of only two eponymous foundations in this book (the other being Whitgift). It was intended by its Founder to be a free school for the poor scholars of the town to provide the education that he had always lacked. Pupils were to be limited to 150 topped up by 'foreigners' if sufficient local pupils could not be found. The foreigners were generally boarders who paid fees and often tended to look down on the poor town boys. The School flourished for the next two hundred years but the Town's opposition to the treatment of the local boys and the restricted curriculum led to a Chancery case. The Court decreed, in 1847, that boarding was to be abolished; thereby cutting numbers to just 31 pupils. R.D. Blackmore, a former scholar at Blundell's (1837-1843) in his novel "*Lorna Doone*", described conditions and customs obtaining at the school in this time.

In 1874, A.L. Francis was appointed Master and in his forty-three years of service he transformed the School and boarding was reinstated. In 1882 the decision was taken to leave the cramped, unhealthy location and move the School to a spacious fifty acre site at Horsdon on the outskirts of Tiverton. The move was paid for from the sale of lands bequeathed by the Founder. As a result and due to the brilliant leadership of Francis, numbers increased to 250 and Blundell's became a First Grade School and was even referred to as the 'Eton of the West'.

BOLTON SCHOOL

Dennis Roxby Bott

Centre Arch and Centre Quad

Bolton School is one of the oldest schools in Lancashire. The origins of the School can be traced back to 1516 and, like all medieval grammar schools, its original purpose was the teaching of Latin.

In 1644, the long association with the Lever name began when Robert Lever endowed the School, by funding its move from the original Tudor buildings to a site next to Bolton Parish Church. There it stayed until 1899 when another and more illustrious Lever, William Hesketh Lever, facilitated the School's move to Westbourne by purchasing a freehold site and financing the necessary alterations. At the same time Bolton Grammar School was merged with Bolton High School for Boys. In 1913, a further merger occurred with the amalgamation of The Boys' School with Bolton High School for Girls and The Bolton School Foundation formally came into existence on 1st April 1915.

The Girls' School had been founded in 1877 when it was one of the very earliest public day schools for girls in Britain. It quickly established a reputation for academic excellence being expertly guided by a series of distinguished Headmistresses including Mrs Sarah Corbett who had been one of the initial intake of students at Girton College Cambridge ; the first residential college for women. Her immediate successors, Miss Vikias and Miss Johnson were graduates from the fledgling Newnham College Cambridge in the 1880s. It is not surprising that Bolton girls began winning places at Cambridge in the 1890s and have continued ever since. The School quickly settled into purpose built premises in Park Road which were described at the time as "the last word in school design"

William Lever's grand design for his newly created co-ed Bolton School, envisaged a U-shaped building with one wing for boys and one for girls. At the apex would be the clock tower. Building began in 1924 on Chorley New Road and was eventually finished in 1965. Dennis Roxby Bott's painting clearly shows the central clock tower and the boys' wing on the right.

William Lever was born in 1851, in Bolton, and was educated at the Bolton Church Institute. Beginning in his father's grocery business he started to manufacture soap from vegetable oils instead of tallow in partnership with his brother James. The company called 'Lever Brothers' was hugely successful and became part of the multinational Unilever PLC.

From 1888 William Lever began to put his philanthropic principles into practice through the construction of Port Sunlight, a model community designed for the workers of Lever Brothers. Amongst his many benefactions are a school of tropical medicine at Liverpool University and the gift of Lancaster House ("the most valuable property in London") to the Nation. He was made a baron in 1917 and became Viscount Leverhulme in 1922. He died in 1925 but his connection with the School is manifested in the School coat of arms granted in 1923. The device of two black diagonal stripes with the edges of the upper one scalloped has been used by the Lever families of Lancashire since The Middle Ages.

BOOTHAM SCHOOL

Dennis Roxby Bott

View of Minster

Bootham School in York is one of Britain's eight Quaker Schools. Although situated almost within the precincts of York Minster, its 17th century Dissenter origins place it outside the Anglican fold.

At the heart of Quaker faith, which has its origins in Christianity, is the belief that we all have something of God within us and consequently religion should reflect this personal experience free from dogma and ritualistic ceremony. Quakers worship in a variety of ways including silent worship and worship led by a Pastor when readings and hymns may be included. However a common characteristic is the example Quakers set by the modest way they live their lives in simple egalitarian and principled testimony.

Quaker is a sobriquet for 'The Religious Society of Friends' founded in England in the late 1640s by George Fox. It received great encouragement from Oliver Cromwell and the Commonwealth because of its Puritan ethos. However the tide turned with the Restoration and Fox and his fellow Dissenters were greatly persecuted. Fox was charged with blasphemy and during the course of his trial Mr Justice Bennet called their Movement's members 'Quakers' "because we bid them tremble at the word of God". Another popular sobriquet is *'Friends'*

Since its beginnings in England Quakerism has spread throughout the world, particularly in the United States where, in 1680, in the face of opposition and persecution, William Penn founded the Commonwealth of Pennsylvania where Friends could settle and practice their faith safely.

A typical Quaker meeting at Bootham School starts with a period of silent worship and is attended by the whole School in a totally unstructured setting with boys and girls of all ages sitting randomly with teachers amongst them. They sit in silence for a full 15 minutes before the Headmaster, without ceremony, concludes proceedings with the usual notices and announcements.

Bootham School was founded in 1823 by The Religious Society of Friends for the sons of Friends (Quakers). The first premises on Lawrence Street in York were leased from the Hospital run by a local Quaker committee. In 1846 the School moved to 20, Bootham and further buildings and land were acquired. In 1891, boys whose parents were not Quakers, were admitted for the first time. In 1899, a serious fire occurred as a result of a science experiment which went wrong. As a consequence, the School had to be rebuilt, but despite the disruption, the School continued to function before it was formally reopened in1902.

Because of its Quaker ethos Bootham developed a 'whole school' approach, with natural and physical sciences being encouraged. At this time, at the end of the 19th century, most prestigious Public Schools were overly concerned with manliness and games. Bootham has produced many distinguished scientists as well as ethical industrialists such as the Rowntree family of chocolate manufacturers. Although today there are only a few Quaker pupils, the school still adheres to many Quaker principles such as equality and searching for "that of God in everyone".

BRADFORD GRAMMAR SCHOOL

Dennis Roxby Bott

Main Building

The origins of Bradford Grammar School are obscure as is the case with many of our schools. The Charter of Incorporation was granted in 1662 by Charles II, but there is incontrovertible evidence that a school possessing property of its own was in existence a century earlier. Circumstantial evidence suggests a school being in existence even earlier.

In 1548 a large parish church was built in Bradford replacing a much smaller one. Analogy suggests that, shortly after this, a necessary concomitant: a grammar school, would have followed. It would have been fully maintained by the Church with the Vicar as Headmaster and the scholars would have been choristers.

In 1553 the School's separate entity was established in a suit at law when Bradford Parish Church fell to the Crown. As a result of the suit the Grammar School property was identified as being separate from the Church property.

In 1818 the School moved from its original site to Manor Row but was not a great success and an alternative Bradford High School was set up in 1860 by Sir Jacob Behrens and others. In 1871 he was responsible for the successful merger of the two schools. The new and improved Bradford Grammar School became a school of the first grade with new buildings being constructed to satisfy increasing demands. A regular stream of candidates gained entrance scholarships to Oxford and Cambridge during the late 19th and early 20th century.

In 1926 it was decided to move the School to Frizinghall, up the Aire Valley, two miles from the centre of Bradford. A public competition was held to select the architect for the new school. From 83 designs, the architect chosen, in 1927, was Edmund Fermoud. However it took another ten years to raise the necessary £150,000 from public subscription.

The School's imposing position on a built up terrace came about due to a mistake in the original specification. The original site plan was incorrectly orientated by 25° which, when corrected in the final working drawing, meant that there was a 25 foot drop in front of the main elevation and entrance. A huge terrace had to be built in front of the School which gave it a most impressive, elevated public face.

The new School was completed in 1939, but before possession could be taken the Second World War broke out and the new buildings were requisitioned by the Army. Considerable damage was done by the soldiers stationed there. It was not until 1949 that a repaired and completed School was opened by the Duke of Edinburgh. However the final result was one of the finest school buildings in the country. In 2002, the Duke of Edinburgh returned to the School to formally open a massive building and refurbishment project.

BRENTWOOD SCHOOL

Hubert Pragnell

Main School

The founder of Brentwood School, Sir Anthony Browne was one of life's great survivors having lived through the greatest period of religious turbulence in English history.

The mid-16th century was a time of great uncertainty, caused by Henry VIII's Reformation. The pendulum swung from Catholic to Protestant and back again and saw no less than five monarchs rule although Lady Jane Grey, the Protestant pretender, lasted for only nine days.

Sir Anthony Browne saw his fortunes wax and wane during this period. In 1553, towards the end of Protestant Edward VI's reign, he was Member of Parliament for Malden and one of the Justices of the Peace for Essex. However he became a victim of the boy King's religious intolerance when he was imprisoned for allegedly misappropriating Church goods. However, after Lady Jane Grey's short reign, the Catholic Mary I came to the throne and, after only a few months imprisonment, Anthony Browne was released and became once again an Essex Justice of the Peace. In this role he became one of 'Bloody Mary's' enforcers.

It is not entirely clear whether Anthony Browne was a practising Catholic – probably. But he was required to take part in the purge of Protestants that took place during Mary's reign. No less than 300 were burnt at the stake nationwide including The Oxford Martyrs: Archbishop Cranmer and Bishops Latimer and Ridley. Browne was to oversee the burning of the 19 year old Protestant Martyr William Hunter at Brentwood. His memorial can be seen outside Brentwood School by Wilson's Corner and the eponymous William Hunter Way.

Browne was lavishly rewarded for his diligent service to Queen Mary when, in 1555, he was appointed Sergeant at Law to the King and Queen. In 1558, in the twilight of her reign, Mary granted Letters Patent to Browne for the foundation of a free Grammar School in Brentwood.

Queen Elizabeth's accession to the throne in 1558 saw a determined effort to heal religious division with none of the excessive religious persecution that had taken place under her siblings' reigns. In fact Anthony Browne prospered greatly during Elizabeth's reign as a result of rendering his great service by producing a definitive Treatise which laid down that Mary Queen of Scots was to be heir apparent in the event of Elizabeth dying without issue. This paved the way for Mary's son James VI of Scotland to succeed to the English Crown in 1601. For this singular service Anthony Brown was knighted in 1567, the year he died.

Anthony Browne wasted no time in founding Brentwood School shortly after Elizabeth acceded to the throne but he died shortly after setting up his Foundation. However his step daughter Dorothy carried on the good work and moved the fledgeling school to its present site and built Big School which remains to this day as the School's 'hub'. It contains a foundation stone inscribed "Dorothy Huddleston 1568".

The Main School was added in 1910 during the reign of Brentwood's most influential Headmaster Edwin Bean (1891-1913).

CANFORD SCHOOL

Dennis Roxby Bott

The View from Mountjoy

Canford School has a truly idyllic setting on the banks of the River Stour. It occupies a 250 acre site which includes Canford Manor and its Great Park. Founded in 1923, it was the third school in the newly created Allied Schools' Group whose driving force was the remarkable Revd Percy Warrington (1889-1961). He was from the evangelical Protestant wing of the Church of England who were worried about the ascendency gained during the 19th century by the Anglo-Catholics within the Church of England, particularly The Woodard Foundation who had created a group of 30 schools. In order to redress the balance, the Revd Percy Warrington, on becoming Secretary of The Church of England Trust in 1918, directed its resources to founding a series of schools and colleges in the evangelical tradition, including St Peter's College in Oxford and Stowe School in Buckingham. Altogether 14 schools were founded and Percy Warrington became a remarkable ecclesiastical entrepreneur.

Percy Warrington acquired Canford Manor from its owner Lord Wimborne, whose grandfather, Sir John Guest, had acquired Canford Manor in 1846. He was the greatest ironmaster in the country as a result of the growth of the railways. His business eventually became the great blue chip company 'Guest, Keen & Nettleford' and his son, Sir Ivor Guest, became the 1st Baron Wimborne in 1880. Sir Ivor's wife, Cornelia, became one of the first Governors of the new school.

Sir John and Lady Charlotte asked Charles Barry (responsible for The Houses of Parliament) to improve upon the house designed by Edward Bloor (responsible for Buckingham Palace and Marlborough College), which had been built twenty years earlier as a replacement for the Jacobean manor. One building was retained from the medieval period: John o'Gaunt's Kitchen which had been built in 1426 as the bedchamber block of the Earl of Salisbury's large manor. Lady Charlotte converted it into the Manor House kitchen.

Charles Barry also designed a museum called 'Nineveh Court' to house some of the archaeological treasures which Lady Charlotte's cousin Henry Layard had discovered while excavating Assyria (present day Iraq). The 3,000 year old antiquities included several massive stone carvings from the throne room of the Assyrian King, Assurnasirpal II (883-859 BC). The antiquities remained undisturbed at Canford until 1919 when most of the collection was sold at public auction and ended up in the New York Metropolitan Museum. The Nineveh Court Museum became the school Tuck Shop and all that remained of the antiquities were plaster cast reproductions which had been heavily painted over. However in 1992 Dr John Russell from Columbia University discovered one of the so called plaster casts was not a reproduction but an original Assyrian frieze. In 1994 it was sold at Christies for $11.8m. A new reproduction is set within a wall of the Tuck Shop.

Canford School has one further distinction: It was, until recently, the only school in Britain to possess a real tennis court built in 1879 by Ivor Guest. The game was much loved by Henry VIII and was the forerunner of lawn tennis. There are, in fact only 50 courts worldwide.

CATERHAM SCHOOL

Dennis Flanders

The School Front

The School was founded in 1811 in Newington in South London by the Revd John Townsend to provide a boarding education for the sons of Congregational Ministers. It moved to new premises in Lewisham in 1815.

By the late 1850s the School was beginning to feel the pinch literally. The new South Eastern Railway had not only acquired some of the School's land but its frequent trains running in close proximity to the School were a great intrusion. Housing development all around the School meant that there could be no expansion of facilities on its Lewisham site.

After many trials and tribulations, the School moved to its present site on 1st October 1884. 114 boys and their teaching staff moved to Caterham and by the end of the century the School accepted sons of laymen and also day boys.

The move to Caterham would not have been possible but for the efforts of one man, The Revd Josiah Viney, the School's 'Second Founder'. As Honorary Secretary for fourteen years and then President, he oversaw the process of seeking and securing a suitable site for the School away from Lewisham.

Another key figure in the School's success was the Headmaster, the Revd Thomas Rudd, who after twenty-five successful years at Lewisham presided over the transition to 'remote' Caterham for a further ten years. He also saw to it that his successors for the next forty years were products of Lewisham. The Rev. Horace Hall 1894-1910 and Allan P Mottram 1910-1934. The latter had been Head Prefect in 1892.

The School is situated in the Harestone Valley on an eighty acre site, in a beautiful setting beneath the North Downs, encircled by a great profusion of trees.

In April 1961 the School celebrated its 150th Anniversary with the publication of *"The Caterham Chronicle,"* a newspaper produced in the style of the early 1800s which received nationwide publicity on the BBC. The Chronicle reported that The Harestone, an ancient conglomerate, had been restored to its former location within the grounds of Caterham School after many years in exile. It weighed two and a half tons and has a circumference of 16 feet. It was probably used as the boundary stone of the old Caterham Manor and is clearly marked on a map dated 1875. Boundary stones were at this time called 'hoar stones' and it is a derivation of this that gave the name 'Harestone', which in turn gives its name to the Harestone Valley.

For many years the stone had resided in the garden of a local resident Mrs A. Berry who kindly agreed to restore it to its original location. The ancient Harestone can be seen quite clearly to the right in Dennis Flanders' painting which was produced in 1991 to commemorate the centenary of the Old Caterhamian Association.

In 2011 the School celebrated its Bicentenary with a service at Westminster Abbey

CHARTERHOUSE

Dennis Roxby Bott

The South African Cloisters

Charterhouse was founded by Sir Thomas Sutton in 1611, on the site of an old Carthusian monastery near Smithfield in London called 'The Charterhouse' (after Chartreux in France where the Order originated). The monastery was closed in 1537 as part of the Dissolution ordered by Henry VIII. Its Prior, John Houghton, was executed for resisting and ten monks also perished, known as 'The Charterhouse Martyrs'. The Charterhouse buildings, including the chapel, became a very grand mansion owned successively by the Duke of Norfolk and the Earl of Suffolk.

In May 1611, Thomas Sutton, who had made his fortune from coal, purchased The Charterhouse from the Earl of Suffolk for £13,000. He died shortly after but had made provision in his Will for the establishment of a hospital for 80 pensioners and a school for 40 boys to be housed at Charterhouse. Thomas Sutton was buried in the chapel.

The School remained in London until 1872 when the Headmaster, Dr Haig Brown, engineered the School's move to Godalming in Surrey. Conditions in London had become cramped and overcrowded. The architect, Philip Charles Hardwick, designed a wonderful collection of Victorian High Gothic buildings incorporating a stone arch from the old school known as 'Gownboy Arch'. The impact on the Goldalming landscape was quite startling.

In 1872, the FA Challenge Cup was inaugurated and was the first knockout competition of its type in the world. It was won by Old Carthusians in 1881 when they beat Eton 3-0 in the Final. This was fitting, since Charterhouse, along with the other major Public Schools, were leading proponents of football in the 19th century, and helped codify the disparate rules governing the game. In 1885 the game became professional, with the amateurs such as Old Carthusians entering a new competition: 'The FA Amateur Cup'. They won this competition twice in 1894 and in 1897. They were the first team to win both cup competitions. Wimbledon FC was the last to emulate this feat in 1988.

Since 1902, Old Carthusians have competed for the Arthur Dunn Cup, a special competition for Old Boys' teams. They have won this competition a record 18 times.

Dennis Roxby Bott's painting depicts the South African Cloisters which commemorate Old Carthusians who died in the Boar War. However there is another war memorial, the largest in England; the Charterhouse School Chapel, which was designed by Giles Gilbert Scott to commemorate nearly 700 Old Carthusians who died in the First World War 1914-1918.

CHEAM SCHOOL

Jane Carpanini

The Loggia from the Formal Garden

Today Cheam School is a leading preparatory school occupying 100 acres at Headley in Hampshire on the Berkshire border near Newbury. As its name suggests, it began life in 1645 at a house in Cheam called 'Whitehall'. The School was founded by the Revd George Aldrich who is reputed to have lived at Whitehall and had for ten years been a curate at St Dunstan's Church in Cheam. The clean downland air attracted pupils from London providing an escape from London's Great Plague of 1665.

In 1719 the School moved to a larger site and a new school was built originally known as 'Manor House School' in Cheam High Street where it remained for over 200 years. The School's most successful Headmaster during these years was William Gilpin who was at the helm from 1752 until 1777 and was succeeded by his son, also William Gilpin, who maintained his father's successful progress. William Snr. was immortalised as 'Doctor Syntax' by the writer William Coombe and the caricaturist William Rowlandson. The Revd Robert Tabor became Headmaster in 1865 when it first became a preparatory school. He in turn was succeeded as Headmaster by his son Arthur. Between them they reigned as Headmasters from 1856–1920 when at some time the name of the school site was changed to 'Tabor Court'. The school buildings were pulled down in 1935.

The School moved to Headley in 1934, when Cheam was developing from a quiet leafy village to a busy suburb with consequent road and building encroachment. The Duke of Edinburgh, Prince Philip was a pupil, and so was his son Charles (Prince of Wales). Whitehall, the original home of the school is now a museum, visited on an annual basis by the younger pupils as a sort of pilgrimage.

Two mergers in the 1990s with Hawtreys and Inhurst House (a girls' school) have helped to establish Cheam as one of the leading co-educational prep. schools in Britain with a mixture of boarders and day students. Nearly a third of pupils in the last two years have gained scholarships and exhibitions to schools such as Marlborough, Winchester, Radley, Wellington, Wycombe Abbey, Cheltenham Ladies' College and Harrow.

Amongst items on display in the School archives are 19th century prints and watercolours of the School when it was located at Tabor Court.

CHELTENHAM COLLEGE

Ken Messer

Chapel and Library

'The Cheltenham Proprietary College', as it was originally known, was the first of seven English Public Schools to be founded at the beginning of Queen Victoria's reign. There was a great demand for education from the newly emerging middle classes enriched and empowered by the Industrial Revolution.

Cheltenham, whilst only a small town, had become fashionable through its sources of natural spa water believed to heal all kinds of illnesses. It attracted a high proportion of middle and upper class parents as residents, with the population growing from 3,000 in 1801 to 35,000 in 1851. Shares in the College were allotted to 650 gentlemen (mere retailers were excluded) who were each entitled to nominate one pupil.

In 1841 Cheltenham Proprietary College commenced life in three houses along Bays Hill Terrace (now The George Hotel) in the centre of town. Within two years it had moved to its present site on the Bath Road, with Boyne House as the first Boarding House. It soon became known simply as 'Cheltenham College'. The two main schoolrooms, Big Classical and Big Modern, were designed in the Perpendicular Gothic style by James Wilson of Bath. This was a departure from the Regency Style which had hitherto been the dominant feature in Cheltenham.

The School was divided into two sides: those in the Military side being trained to move on to Sandhurst or Woolwich for a career in the army, whilst those in the Classical side were educated for university entrance. By 1880 Cheltenham was the second largest school in Britain and reckoned to be one of the ten Great Public Schools. In 1865 a Junior Department was added to the main College

buildings and in 1909 Cheltenham College Junior School opened on Thirlestaine Road. Both schools remained boarding and day for boys until 1981 when the first girls' house opened.

The first chapel, in use from 1858 until 1896, had been designed by D.J. Humphris of Cheltenham. It was never consecrated, being too small, and facing the wrong way (North / South instead of East / West). To celebrate the Jubilee of Cheltenham College in 1891, a new chapel was to be built. The architect was selected by running a competition, and Henry Prothero, an Old Cheltonian, was chosen. The New Chapel, completed and dedicated in 1896, is one of the most magnificent school chapels anywhere. Its soaring architecture and fan vaulting are reminiscent of King's College Cambridge and it is genuinely considered, by present and past students, to be the heart of the College. After 1896 the Old Chapel became first the Library and then the Dining Hall, with the library being housed in Big Modern.

Although there has been no military bias in the curriculum for over 60 years, fourteen Old Cheltonians have received the Victoria Cross. The College still has a very active Combined Cadet Force and retains strong links with the armed services. It is the only Public School, other than Eton, to have its own colours. Distinguished OCs include Major General Sir Michael Rose, UK Special Forces; the Antarctic explorer Dr Edward Wilson; BBC Reporter Rageh Omaar; and Lindsay Anderson, the film director who made the somewhat controversial film " If " at the school.

CHRIST COLLEGE, BRECON

Dennis Flanders

The School Chapel

The 16th century was a time of great activity in education. After the Dissolution of the Monasteries in 1538, although some of the Church property went into private hands, much of it was dedicated to the use of education. Under Henry VIII, many new schools were given new charters or re-endowed as King's Schools. This period coincided with a time when Henry VIII brought all of Wales under his control, creating new Welsh counties including Breconshire. This combination of events resulted in the 1541 foundation of 'The College of Christ of Brecknock' to provide education in the area and thus would "the Welsh rudeness" soon be framed to English civility.

Before the Dissolution, Christ College had been a Dominican Friary founded in about 1250 and many buildings survive from this period. The Chapel and Dining Hall are both still in daily use, having been restored by the ubiquitous George Gilbert Scott in the 19th century.

Like many schools founded in the 16th century, Christ College suffered dramatic changes of fortune. The maintenance of the buildings was a constant struggle given that the original endowment was not overly generous; and the reluctance of prebendaries, the Bishops of St David's to pass on endowed incomes to the School.

The English Civil War of the 17th century caused devastation and although Bishop Lucy carried out some repairs after 1660, by the middle of the 19th century the buildings were in a ruinous state and pupil numbers were few.

A new start was imperative: A committee of local landowners, clergy and businessmen came to the rescue and the School was re-founded by Act of Parliament in 1855. New buildings were needed and the Llandaff diocesan architects, Pritchard and Seddon, designed the present School House, Donaldson House, and the 'Big School' (now the library).

Christ College is particularly proud of its fine cricketing tradition. Until fairly recently it played host each year to the touring Test Match sides; its cricket pitch is considered to be the finest in Wales.

When Dennis Flanders had almost completed his painting in 1991 it was pointed out that he had omitted the small but significant squint windows along the side of the Chapel. These were the facility by which the 16th century lepers could observe the services without fear of contaminating the congregation.

CITY OF LONDON SCHOOL

Dennis Flanders

New School 1986

The School's origins date back to 1442 and a bequest left by one John Carpenter, Town Clerk of London, to educate four poor men's sons. They were attached to the Chapel of the Guildhall whose library Carpenter had helped to found. He was a friend and Executor of Dick Whittington and codified the laws, customs and privileges of the City in his *"Liber Albus"*.

In 1536, The Guildhall Chapel was suppressed as part of Henry VIII's Reformation and 'Carpenter's children' led a wandering existence and ended up in, 1826, at Tonbridge School.

By 1834, however, Carpenter's endowment had increased so much in value that the Corporation of London decided to build its own educational establishment. After receiving assent by Act of Parliament the new City of London School (CLS) was opened in 1837 on Milk Street off Cheapside. It was to cater for 500 boys and, unusually for this time, there were to be no religious tests for either boys or masters. A wonderful example of religious tolerance in education, which proved to be a wise move because fresh scholarships flowed from the eclectic City. During the time at Milk Street the School developed a reputation for excellence in mathematics and science.

By 1882 conditions in Milk Street had become cramped but unlike other Public Schools who left London for more spacious surroundings, CLS stayed in the City. Its identity was inextricably linked to the City of London, so a new site was found on the Thames Embankment. The new, much larger, school was designed by Architects Davis and Emmanuel and provides accommodation for over 600 boys.

The School had special entry arrangements for choristers from the Temple since 1900 and The Chapel Royal, St James's Palace, since 1926. In 1927 Ernest Lough's recording of *"Oh for the Wings of a Dove"* sung by the Choir of CLS, was the first record to sell a million copies.

As educational needs changed, so extensions to the buildings were added but, by the time another century had passed, it was obvious that a third set of purpose–built premises were required. Once again moving out of London was unthinkable, and, luckily, a site between St Paul's Cathedral and the River Thames became available. (The goodwill of the City no doubt oiling the wheels). It was situated only a few hundred yards to the east of the old School on the other side of Blackfriars Bridge. The old School was sold to American bankers, J.P. Morgan, for use as prestigious offices. Fortunately, being a listed building, the façade could not be altered.

The new School, designed by T. Meddings and opened in 1986, was built on the site of Baynards Castle which was used as a royal palace by Edward IV, Richard III and Henry VII. It was also the residence of three Queens of Henry VIII: Catherine of Aragon, Anne Boleyn and Anne of Cleves.

CLIFTON COLLEGE

Clifford Bayly

Big School

The middle to late 19th century saw a great demand from the newly emerging middle classes for new and progressive schools with a Christian ethos.

In 1862 Clifton College was founded by a group of merchants and professional people to reflect the needs of Bristol's bustling commercial activity, its cultural life and its University. Situated in the salubrious residential suburb of Clifton, its prestigious location is enhanced by the presence of Brunel's Clifton Suspension Bridge which spans the Avon Gorge. It is said that the Clifton area grew because there was a Public School nearby. Next door is the Zoo which has also expanded.

The Victorian drive and self-confidence was exhibited throughout Britain in its public buildings and institutions. Nowhere is this better illustrated than the wonderful edifice that is Clifton College. Seen from across the grassy sward of the Close, the Chapel; Big School and Library; School House and the arcaded Percival Building have an architectural integrity that is remarkable: Victorian mock Gothic in all its glory. Even later building such as the 1927 Science Schools have the same unity of design. The College buildings were designed by architect Charles Hansom and his son Edward and erected between 1862-1875, although the Wilson Tower was not added until 1890. The homogenous warm local sandstone of the buildings is wonderfully interrupted by what John Betjeman describes as 'something magnificent': a chapel designed in 1909 by Sir Charles Nicholson, crowned with a copper lantern (now attractively green with age), in the manner of Ely Cathedral.

The first Head Master, the Revd John Percival, had been an assistant master at Rugby; it was the desire of the founders to have a school modelled on Dr Arnold's Rugby. However Percival was no pale imitation of Arnold and in his own way was ahead of his time. In the 1860s, he introduced science, a revolutionary move when it is considered that it had not for long been a degree subject at Oxford and Cambridge. By 1877, science was taught to 90 per cent of boys. A distinguished line of scientists emerged from Clifton including Nobel Prize winners Sir Nevill Mott and Sir John Kendrew. In 1878 Percival took the bold step of providing a boarding house known as 'Polacks' for the Anglo-Jewish community. This continued until 2005.

In June 1899 on the College's cricket ground, The Close, the highest individual cricket score ever recorded '628 not out' was reached by A.E.J. Collins (who sadly was killed in the First World War.) The Close played an important role in the history of cricket as a witness to thirteen of W.G. Grace's first class hundreds for Gloucestershire in the County Championship. Grace's two sons attended the College.

A poignant architectural feature on College Road is the Memorial Arch designed by Charles Holden. Its dedication in 1922 was attended by Field-Marshal Douglas Haig, an Old Cliftonian, who commanded the British Expeditionary Force in the First World War (a statue of Haig stands just behind the arch). Another Old Cliftonian, Sir Henry Newbolt in his immortal poem " *Vitaï Lampada*" drew together the strands of cricket endeavour and war time inspiration: "There's a breathless hush on the Close tonight......Play up and play the game"

CRANLEIGH SCHOOL

Dennis Roxby Bott

South Entrance and Chapel

Cranleigh's foundation in 1865 was the result of the combined inspiration of two remarkable men, the Revd Canon Henry Sapte, Rector of Cranleigh and later Archdeacon of Surrey, and Sir George Cubitt, the local Squire. Henry Sapte had earlier raised funds to build England's first Cottage Hospital in the Village. Sir George was the son of a successful London property developer and architect, Arthur Cubitt, and he donated most of the two hundred acres which make up the present Cranleigh School campus. Sir George later became the 1st Baron Ashcombe of Bodiham.

Henry Woodyer, born in Guildford in 1816, was chosen to be the architect to build the school which was first known as 'The Surrey County School'. After Eton, Woodyer studied at Merton College, Oxford and became a follower of the High Church 'Oxford Movement' led by Keble, Pusey and Newman. A leading adherent of the Movement at the time was William Butterfield, a young and serious minded architect who became the 'darling' of many High Church societies. Henry Woodyer was greatly attracted to Butterfield's work and became a pupil of his for a short while. They worked closely on a number of projects including the magnificent medieval church of Ottery St Mary in Devon. Butterfield's iconic masterpiece was the controversial Keble College Chapel completed in 1876, which represented the living enbodiment of the Oxford Movement's principles.

Henry Woodyer's original designs for Cranleigh School included a quadrangle and chapel, although only the south and east sides of the quadrangle were completed (at a cost of just under £12,000) in time for the School's opening in 1865. The north and west sides of the quad followed three years later, along with a clock tower finished in 1870, although the clock itself did not appear until 1874.

The Chapel of the Holy Infant was added in 1869, at a further cost of £5,500. This sum was donated in its entirety by another local benefactor, Sir Henry Peek, in memory of his mother whose family had fled France to escape religious persecution following the revoking of the Edict of Nantes. The Chapel is in the early English decorated style, and is built with red bricks interlined with bands of Mansfield stone and black brick. In many ways it can be seen as a forerunner in design of the Keble College Chapel which was built seven years later. A restoration process was launched in the Chapel in 2009, inspired by the construction of a new £600,000 Mander Organ, the gift of a generous Old Cranleighan, Hamish Ogston.

The most recent addition to the buildings at Cranleigh is an Academic Centre named after a former Headmaster, David Emms. The Emms Centre cost just over £10,000,000 and is home to some high-tech facilities for Science, Maths and Modern Languages.

CULFORD SCHOOL

Clifford Bayly

The Iron Bridge

Although John Wesley founded his first Methodist school at Kingswood Bath in 1748 it was not until the latter part of the 19th century that the Methodist Independent Schools Group was founded to actively promote the opening of further Methodist schools. The first of the new schools was 'The Leys School' in Cambridge in 1875 followed by, in 1881, 'The East Anglian School for Boys', the original name for Culford School. Initially, the School was located in the centre of Bury St Edmunds where it remained for fifty years. Today there are sixteen independent Methodist schools in the British Isles.

In 1935 the School moved four miles north of Bury St Edmunds to Culford Park latterly the home of the 7th Earl of Cadogan and thereafter became known as 'Culford School'. The old school premises on Thingoe Hill became home to a new school 'The East Anglian School for Girls' which in 1972 moved to Culford to create one of the first co-educational schools in Britain.

Culford School's setting in 480 acres of parkland is truly magnificent as are the illustrious former inhabitants of Culford Hall. After the Coote family had initially acquired the Hall from the Abbey at Bury St Edmunds, courtesy of the Reformation, it passed to Sir Nicholas Bacon in 1586. He was Chancellor of the Exchequer to Queen Elizabeth I and an extremely wealthy man. He demolished the old manor house and built a new one very much in the Tudor style with red brick gables and bay windows. In the middle was a courtyard open to the sky.

In 1659 Culford Hall was inherited by Sir Frederick Cornwallis whose family's long association with Culford lasted 164 years. Its most distinguished family member was Charles Cornwallis (1738 – 1805) the 1st Marquis who served his country with distinction in four theatres of war. He was successful in three campaigns in Europe, India and Ireland but, sadly, he is most remembered for his one significant defeat: the Battle of Yorktown in Virginia where he was forced to surrender to General George Washington, the turning point in the American War of Independence.

Despite these heavy overseas commitments, he still found time to make major changes to Culford Hall. Samuel Wyatt was engaged in 1889 to give the place a facelift. This involved cladding the red bricks with white mathematical tiles, removing the bay windows and covering the courtyard with a glass dome. At the same time the grounds were landscaped by Humphrey Repton who created a lake fed by the River Culford. To span the lake, Wyatt built a bridge made from cast iron, a very new innovation at the time. Only recently has it been recognised as one of the most important bridges of this period. It is thought to be the fifth oldest iron bridge in the world and is now Grade 1 listed.

After the death of the 2nd Marquis Cornwallis in 1823, the estate was purchased by the Benyon family who, in 1889, sold it to the 5th Earl of Cadogan. Great changes were made between 1894 -1900 including an Italianate Cupola disguising the Water Tower. Finally, in 1935, the Methodist Board of Education bought Culford Hall and it is undoubtedly the jewel in its crown.

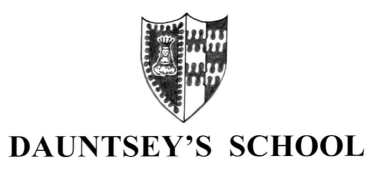

DAUNTSEY'S SCHOOL

Jane Carpanini

Main Building

Dauntsey's School in West Lavington, Wiltshire, was founded by William Dauntsey in 1553. It is another example of a school founded by a local lad, who made his fortune in the City of London. He became Master of The Mercers' Livery Company, who are number one in Livery Company order of precedence.

In his Will, William Dauntsey left his London properties in trust to The Mercers' Company on condition they applied its benefits to the founding of almshouses and a school in his native West Lavington. The original school building still stands opposite the church in the High Street of West Lavington. Not a great deal is known about the school from the 16th century until the late 19th century.

However, in 1878, the inhabitants of West Lavington formed a Committee of Investigation into the way the School was being run by The Mercers' Company. The major grievance was the allegation that only a small proportion of the annual revenue from William Dauntsey's estate was being applied towards running the school and maintaining its buildings. Other grievances highlighted the use of school buildings and land for commercial and not scholastic purposes.

It is no coincidence that this local uprising followed a national campaign led by two Birmingham MPs, the Rt Hon Joseph Chamberlain and Jesse Collings, to make education more freely available to the masses and to look at the way endowed schools were administered. The National Education League, which was founded in 1869, and The Endowed Schools Commission of 1874 were the catalysts for change at Dauntsey. In fact, Joseph Chamberlain, the President of the Board of Trade, led negotiations with The Mercers' Company to refound the School and finance its move to a new site with new buildings. Jesse Collings

was crucial as advisor to Chamberlain because he had a passionate interest in both education and agricultural reform. What emerged from these negotiations was a new school to be called 'The Dauntsey Agricultural School', with eight of the twenty three governors coming from The Mercers' Company. The impressive new school building, designed by architect Fred Ponting, was erected on a newly acquired twelve acre site known as 'Planks' ground. Appropriately, the new Dauntsey Agricultural School was opened by the Rt Hon Joseph Chamberlain on the 7th May 1895.

In the 20th century the School prospered, under George Olive's headmastership (1919–1955) when many new buildings and facilities were added most notably the Manor Estate in 1929 (now the Junior Boarding House). During the 1920s the School's second great benefactor, Samuel Farmer, made many generous donations before his death in 1926.

In 1930 the name was shortened to 'Dauntsey's School' although agriculture remained an important part of the curriculum.

An unusual feature for a land-locked school is its ownership of the 'Jolie Brise', a 56ft gaff cutter originally built in 1913. Acquired by the School in 1977, it is moored on the Hamble, 64 miles to the south in Hampshire. Since 2000, Jolie Brise, crewed by Dauntsey's pupils, has competed in many Tall Ships races, winning the second leg of the Transatlantic Challenge in 2009 and the Tall Ships Race Series 2011.

DENSTONE COLLEGE

Jane Carpanini

The Cricket Match

Denstone College at Uttoxeter in Staffordshire was opened in 1873 and was originally called 'St Chad's College'. It was the fourth school to be opened by Nathaniel Woodard's Anglican Woodard Foundation and the first outside Sussex where Lancing, Hurstpierpoint and Ardingly had opened some years earlier. In all, Woodard opened eleven schools before his death in 1891. The Woodard Foundation has since opened 29 further schools and remains the largest group of Independent Schools in Britain. All of his earlier schools had the overriding characteristic of being strongly Anglo-Catholic, no doubt reflecting the deep impression the tractarian 'Oxford Movement' of Keble, Pusey and Newman, made on him when he was a student at Magdalen Hall Oxford (which later became Hertford College in the 1830s.)

The first buildings of the new school, including the chapel, were designed in the ecclesiastical Gothic style by William Slater and Richard Herbert Carpenter. The latter's father, Richard Cromwell Carpenter, had, in 1848, designed the first Woodward school, Lancing College, in the same Gothic style with its famous cathedral-like chapel.

The foundation of Denstone College was greatly assisted by the local Squire, Sir Thomas Percival Heywood, whose family were wealthy bankers. He had earlier built the local parish church and school. He gifted the land on which Denstone College was built and was it's first Bursar.

Denstone College has a unique distinction for a school in the field of scientific exploration; carrying out the most extensive survey of Inaccessible Island in the South Atlantic. A group of 16 teachers and pupils led by Michael Swales sailed to the island, landing on 25th October 1982 and remaining until 9th February 1983. The members of the expedition managed to ring 3,000 birds during their stay and produced seventeen research papers.

Inaccessible Island is an extinct volcano covering 5 square miles rising out of the South Atlantic Ocean, 28 miles south west of Tristan da Cunha. Both are territories of the United Kingdom although Inaccessible Island unlike Tristan da Cunha has never had a permanent population. It is a protected wildlife reserve which has been designated a World Heritage Site by Unesco.

Denstone College has a proud cricket tradition and at the time Jane Carpanini painted the view opposite the England Under 19 cricket captain was a pupil. Jane's closely observed portrait of an intense game of cricket is a remarkable achievement considering that she had never watched a cricket match before.

DOLLAR ACADEMY

Clifford Bayly

Dewar and Playfair Building

Dollar Academy is Britain's oldest co-educational boarding school. Its 70-acre campus is set at the foot of the Ochil Hills in the small town of Dollar (population 2850), thirteen miles north-east of Stirling. Nearby is Castle Campbell, the traditional lowland home of the Campbell Clan. The castle was originally called Castle Gloom and it is ironical that two burns, Care and Sorrow, run nearby.

The School's founder was Captain McNabb, a native of Dollar, who came from humble origins. He was a herd-boy who left home to go to sea at an early age and by the time he died, in 1802, he had become a rich ship-owner. On his death, he bequeathed a legacy of some £60,000 (equivalent to several million pounds today) to build a 'charity or school' in his native Dollar. There was much dispute over the terms of McNabb's legacy; was the school to be only for the poor children of the parish or was the intake to be wider both economically and geographically? In 1815, the Revd Dr Andrew Mylne was appointed parish minister – he would later also be the School's first Rector. He persuaded the Court of Chancery to accept the wider remit for the school and the potential for a great school was created.

In 1818, Dr Mylne engaged the eminent architect, William Playfair, who designed a magnificent building with a splendid Doric façade. Playfair was also responsible for two of Edinburgh's finest buildings: the Royal Scottish Academy and the National Gallery; both in the same Doric style as Dollar Academy.

Teaching began in 1818 but it was 1821 before the doors of the new 'Dollar Institution' were opened. At its centenary in 1918, it was renamed Dollar Academy, which was much more in keeping with its classical appearance. 'Academy' has connotations with Greek philosophy and by the end of the 19th century it had become very much a Scottish characteristic to call its leading schools 'Academies'.

Dollar, like all educational foundations, has had its vicissitudes, particularly in 1921 when it ran into financial difficulties and was temporarily administered by the County Council. Former pupils came to the rescue by raising funds and creating a further endowment to enable the school to regain its independence in 1934. Disaster struck in 1961 when fire burnt out the interior of the Playfair Building, destroying the fine Library and some 12,000 books. The local population rallied round and temporary accommodation was provided in local halls, Harviestoun Castle and even private houses. Whilst Playfair's façade remained intact, the interior had to be completely rebuilt, and was officially reopened in 1966.

In the early 1930s, John McNabb's coffin was found in the crypt of a disused Meeting House at Mile End in London. The remains were cremated and his ashes were placed in a niche above the famous Bronze Doors of the academy which he founded.

ELLESMERE COLLEGE

Jane Carpanini

The Terraces

Ellesmere College, opened in 1884 and dedicated to St Oswald, was Nathaniel Woodard's ninth school in his Anglican Woodard Foundation. He was, at the time, Sub Dean of Manchester Cathedral. Canon Woodard's religious principles were central to the philosophy of the schools he founded. He wanted his schools to be redoubts of Christian values in the increasingly materialistic world of Victorian England. By the time he died in 1891, he had founded eleven schools. A further twenty nine have since been added.

Set in a delectable landscape of seventy acres and ringed by a glittering necklace of meres in Shropshire's 'Lake District', it is the topographical jewel in the Woodard crown. A broad stretch of immaculate turf on its south western side rises to a spacious terrace on which sits the handsome late Gothic façade of the College's main buildings. With its clock and its long range of dormer windows, it looks out over miles of unspoilt countryside to the distant hills of Wales.

The original College buildings were designed by architects, Carpenter and Inglelow, as an H Plan with three sided quadrangles open to the east and west. The Hall was added in 1897 to an original design by Sir Aston Webb and

partners. A devastating fire in 1966 meant that the hall and chapel had to be reconstructed under the supervision of architects Colcutt & Hamp.

Ellesmere has a strong music tradition where currently over 30% of the pupils learn a musical instrument. It possesses two of the finest organs in the country. The Chapel contains a grand Norman, Hill and Beard organ built in 1968 and made famous far beyond Ellesmere by Brian Runnet's recording of the Hindemith organ sonatas. In 1981 the College acquired a second organ; a renowned veteran of 1864 by the German builder Edmund Schulze, whose organs are esteemed for their deep purple velvety sound. A true Rolls Royce amongst organs, it has pride of place in a new gallery in the hall beneath the third largest hammer – beam roof in England.

As Jane Carpanini's painting, showing a cricket match in progress, illustrates, sport is an important part of the curriculum at Ellesmere. Ellesmere boasts international standards in its academy sports of rugby, cricket, tennis, swimming and shooting.

ETON COLLEGE
John Doyle

School Yard

History has always regarded Henry VI as a feckless monarch; the Lancastrian loser in the Wars of the Roses. However, his most enduring legacies are to be found in the field of education; Eton College founded in 1440 and King's College Cambridge founded a year later. He was determined to create a twin foundation that would surpass what William of Wykeham had achieved when he created his two interrelated foundations; New College Oxford and Winchester College, sixty years earlier. Until the late 19th century, entry to King's College Cambridge was restricted to Old Etonians.

Eton was chosen as the location for his new school by Henry VI because it was close to his castle at Windsor. It was the first Great School to be founded by a monarch and, as a consequence, the most richly endowed. A later monarch, George III, also became closely associated with the School, so much so that his birthday, the 4th of June, is still celebrated as a holiday. Because of this royal patronage, Eton became the favourite place of education for the sons of rich or noble parents. It is not surprising that Etonians have always occupied high positions in public offices. Nineteen former pupils have become British Prime Ministers.

Like Winchester, Eton's early statutes provided for the education of seventy scholars free of charge. These were supplemented over the years, by large numbers of pupils who paid their own expenses, not in college like the Scholars, but outside the college walls in the town of Eton. As a result they became known as 'Oppidans' from the Latin 'oppidanus' meaning 'town dweller'.

The Oppidans today number over 1240, whilst the King's Scholars remain at around seventy. Entry for King's Scholars is by competitive examination for boys aged 12 to 14, who need apply only a few weeks beforehand and, if successful, may be exempt from paying any fees. King's Scholars live in College, a separate House within the precincts, but join the rest of the School for all activities. These days, around 200 of the Oppidans have their fees reduced by scholarships and bursaries which are means tested.

In sport, Eton has many claims to fame. The proximity of the Thames has enabled Eton to become known as the 'cradle of rowing' in England. The development of football or the variant we know today as 'soccer' owes much to Eton. The F.A. Cup was first awarded in 1872 and the Old Etonians have won the cup twice, in 1879 and 1882, and been four times runners up, before the professional game took over. Two forms of football peculiar to Eton are still played: 'The Field Game', a mixture of rugby and soccer and of course the mudlark known as 'The Wall Game'.

Architecturally Eton is stunning; its chapel is one of the finest examples of the English Perpendical style. John Doyle's painting shows Lupton's Tower, built in 1520 and named after Roger Lupton who was Provost at the time, whilst centre left can be seen the statue of the founder, Henry VI.

FETTES COLLEGE

James Porteous Wood

Founders Day

At first sight there would appear to be nothing to connect a Grand Tour of Europe in the winter of 1814 -15 with the opening of Fettes College in the autumn of 1870. However the two events are directly connected: for it was while he was engaged on the Grand Tour that 27 year old William Fettes, the only child of Sir William Fettes, fell ill and died of typhoid fever. With no prospect of establishing a dynasty, (Sir William was sixty five in 1815) he did by his Will bequeath £166,000 for the establishment of a school in memory of his son.

Sir William Fettes was a grocer by trade and had made his fortune out of a contract to provision the army camps in Scotland during the Napoleonic Wars. He died in 1836, but it was not until 1870 that the school opened. This delay was due to procrastination on the part of Sir William's Trustees, who were concerned about the poor reputation similar hospital schools had acquired. Those set up by other rich Edinburgh citizens, such as George Heriot and Daniel Stewart, were producing, according to a School's Inspector "children who were dishonest, selfish and intellectually inert". The barbaric reputation gained by the great English Public Schools in the 18th and early 19th century did not help.

However, the work of Thomas Arnold at Rugby School had, by the 1840s, shown that boarding schools could be civilised communities. With Arnold's model in mind, the Fettes Trustees decided, in 1864, to proceed with the building of Fettes College. Fortunately, prudent investment of Sir William's original legacy had increased its value to £480, 000 (about £ 45 million in today's money).

The Trustees asked William Playfair , the key architect of the 'Athens of the North' movement, to design their new school with a classical style in mind. However, he died soon after, so David Bryce was appointed and his design was very different. He created a masterpiece in a style that was Scottish Baronial mixed with French Chateau. It certainly had its detractors at the time but is now accepted as one of Scotland's greatest buildings.

The next step in ensuring the College's success was to appoint a headmaster who would replicate Thomas Arnold's template in Scotland. Alexander William Potts had exactly the right pedigree; educated at Shrewsbury and St John's College Cambridge, he had teaching experience at Charterhouse and, most importantly, Rugby where he was Sixth Form Master. His reign at Fettes lasted from 1870 until 1889 and he must rank amongst the greatest of British Headmasters in the Victorian era.

Whilst Fettes can legitimately claim a British Prime Minister, Tony Blair, amongst its alumni, the position of James Bond is ambiguous. In one of the James Bond novels *"You Only Live Twice"* Ian Fleming states the spy attended Fettes College , his father's old school, after being removed from Eton. However there was a real life James Bond who did attend Fettes. He was a frogman with the Special Boat Service thus having a naval background like his fictional namesake. The College has a somewhat elitist reputation and is sometimes referred to as 'Eton in kilts'.

FOREST SCHOOL

Dennis Roxby Bott

Chapel Quad

Forest School is set in a clearing in Epping Forest ten miles to the north east of London near Walthamstow. It was founded in 1834 as 'Forest Proprietary School' whose main purpose was to make a profit for its shareholders. Initially this was achieved with numbers reaching 80 by the end of its first decade. Then major problems arose because of falling numbers due to a reputation rapidly gained for the cruel punishment inflicted by tutors on their pupils. The school nearly closed on several occasions and was clearly no longer profitable.

The year 1848 saw the arrival at Forest of its first great Headmaster, John Gilderdale. He became the School's sole proprietor and changed its name to 'Forest School'. Gilderdale gave the school credibility and stability during his nine years as Headmaster. It is a fitting tribute to the qualities he bought to Forest that the School Chapel was built in 1857, at the very end of his career. Perhaps his greatest legacy to Forest was to allow his daughter, Rebecca, to marry Frederick Barlow Guy, a fellow Yorkshireman and also the son of his own tutor from Howden School, the Revd Thomas Guy. Thus began an eighty three year association between Forest School and the Guy family.

Dr Frederick Barlow Guy was Headmaster of Forest from 1857 until 1886, during which time Forest attained many of its greatest achievements. He introduced the Shakespeare play as a Forest tradition; he built the first swimming pool; the first gymnasium; enlarged the Chapel and, in his final year, the foundation stone of The Memorial Dining Hall was laid. He was also responsible for establishing Forest's association with William Morris, poet, artist, designer

and socialist. Dr Guy was William Morris' private tutor from 1851–1853 when he was Assistant Master at Forest School. He was successful in helping Morris to matriculate to Exeter College, Oxford. They remained lifelong friends and William Morris designed Forest School's Banner as well as producing three stained glass windows for the Chapel designed by Edward Burne-Jones. Two were unfortunately destroyed by flying bombs in 1944. The sledging flag of former pupil Surgeon - Captain Edward Atkinson, a member of Scott's Antartic Expedition hangs at the north end of the Dining Hall.

On his retirement in 1886, Dr Guy's eldest son Thomas became Forest's fifth Headmaster until, after only eight years, he decided to become a Parish Priest in Yorkshire. His brother Ralph more than made up for Thomas's brevity by becoming Forest's sixth and longest serving Headmaster. His reign lasted 40 years until 1935 when he sold the School and went into retirement bringing to an end the Guy Dynasty.

In 1947 the Forest School became a Public School, when its owner and Headmaster, Gerald Miller, made over the school to a non-profit making association. In 1983 John Gough became Head of the School but his title was changed to 'Warden' to reflect the wider responsibilities involved in overseeing three schools including a girls' school opened in 1981, where the pupils are taught separately until merged with the boys at 6th Form level.

GEORGE HERIOT'S SCHOOL

James Porteous Wood

Heriot's Hospital

Located in Lauriston Place on the ridge above Edinburgh's Grassmarket is the great 17th century Scottish Renaissance edifice known as George Heriot's School.

George Heriot's Foundation was set up in 1628, four years after his death. His only sons had perished in an accident at sea, so there were few bequests. Instead he left the bulk of his estate to set up a trust which would found a hospital to care for the "puir paitherless bairns" of Edinburgh. The term 'hospital' was at this time a euphemism for this kind of charitable school. The amount left in this way amounted to £25,000; equivalent to around £20,000,000 in today's money.

The construction of Heriot's Hospital was begun in 1628, by William Wallace. After his death the work was carried on by Master Mason, William Aytoum. The first part of the building, minus the central tower, was completed in the 1640s, just in time to be occupied by Oliver Cromwell's English force during the invasion of Scotland; the building was used as a barracks with horses stabled in the Chapel.

The School finally opened in 1659, after General Monck, on the death of Cromwell, authorised the return of the building to its Governors. It was not until 1693 that the central tower was built to a design by Sir William Bruce and the magnificent façade of Heriot's was complete.

Built using sandstone from Rovelston and with influences from Linlithgow Palace, Heriot's Hospital was the first completely 'regular' design for a building in Scotland with four ranges arranged around a courtyard and corner towers.

In 1693 the Master Mason Robert Mylne added further buildings including The Great Hall, Council Room and Chapel. Finally, he erected a statue of George Heriot in the north quadrangle.

George Heriot (1563 – 1624) rose to prominence in the court of King James VI. He was the court goldsmith and became very wealthy from this position and wealthier still by lending money back to the King and the rest of his Court. As a result of his wealth he became known in Edinburgh as 'Jingling George'. He moved to London along with the Court of James I at the time of the Union of Crowns in 1603 and remained in London until his death in 1624. Although married twice, no legitimate children survived him.

His lasting legacy will always be George Heriot's School but the School provided funds for the establishment of an institution which, after merging with the Watt Institute, (named after James Watt) became Heriot Watt University in 1966.

GLASGOW ACADEMY

James Porteous Wood

Main School Building

Founded in 1845, The Glasgow Academy is the oldest independent school in Glasgow. It was established by members of the newly formed Free Church of Scotland to provide an education based upon strictly evangelical principles and pervaded by religious instruction.

Glasgow Academy was initially located in Elmbank Place but in 1878 moved to a new building at Kelvinbridge. The architect for the new school building was Hugh Barclay, of Messrs H & D Barclay, a Glasgow firm who, over a period of eighty years, designed over 40 schools as well as many churches and commercial buildings. Its finest school was The Glasgow Academy. Its prominent position overlooking the River Kelvin in the heart of Glasgow's affluent suburbs of Kelvinside and Hillhead greatly aided its rapid success.

The Academy's first Rector had been in office only four years when it was decided that the schoolmasters would collectively run the Academy themselves on a collegiate basis without a Rector. This experiment lasted for ten years before Donald Morrison was appointed Rector and oversaw the move to Kelvinside. He remained Rector for 38 years.

In 1919 the War Memorial Trust was established to take over ownership of the Academy and to commemorate those who had served and fallen in the First World War. The merger with Westbourne Girls School in 1990 turned the Academy into a co-educational school and further mergers have followed as the Academy has extended its borders beyond Kelvinside into Milngavie and Newlands.

In 1996 a school tartan was designed by Alison Bruce. The tartan is a combination of the main school colours; navy blue and heather (purple) with the addition of black to give depth.

Notable Alumni include J.M. Barrie, writer of *"Peter Pan"*, Sir Jeremy Isaacs, Founder of Channel 4; Sir James Lithgow, shipbuilder & industrialist; John Reith, 1st Baron Reith, founder of the BBC, James Prime, keyboard player for Deacon Blue and lecturer at the University of the West of Scotland. Another alumnus, Donald Dewar, became in 1999 the first holder of the office of First Minister of Scotland in the new Scottish Parliament.

GRESHAM'S

John Doyle

Big School

Sir John Gresham was a member of The Mercers' Livery Company and on four occasions was its Master. However in 1555, a year before he died, he made The Fishmongers' Livery Company Trustees of his newly founded Gresham School in his home town of Holt, Norfolk. He had not fallen out with The Mercers', it was simply administrative expediency; The Mercers had recently been given the Trusteeship of the newly founded St Paul's School by Sir John Colet, Dean of St Paul's. As the Dutch humanist Erasmus remarked at the time, the Liveries were seen to be men of great probity and containing less corruption than any other organisations including the Church. The Fishmongers were 4th in order in precedence amongst the Great Twelve Livery Companies (The Mercers were ranked 1st).

Gresham's replaced an earlier school, operated under the aegis of the Augustan Priory at Beeston Regis, which was dissolved by Henry VIII in 1539. Gresham and his two brothers, William and Richard, probably attended this local school.

The Fishmongers continue to be associated with the running of the School and seven of the Governors are representatives from The Worshipful Company of Fishmongers, with the Prime Warden being ex-officio.

For 350 years, the School was based in what is now called the 'Old School House', the former Manor House of Holt overlooking the Market Place in the town centre.

In the early 1900s, under an ambitious new headmaster, George Howson, (previously at Uppingham School) the School expanded on to a new campus of some 200 acres at the eastern edge of town. The new School was designed by the architect Mr H. Chatfeild Clarke and includes Big School shown in John Doyle's painting opposite. The original Old School House is now the home of Gresham's Pre-Prep School.

The ubiquitous grasshopper is now the School's logo replacing the coat of arms commemorating the founder Sir John Gresham whose family crest it was. The grasshopper is a heraldic rebus on the name Gresham ('gres' being Middle English for 'grass'). However according to legend, the Gresham progenitor was a foundling discovered in long grass by the presence of a grasshopper. The Gresham Grasshopper is also used by Gresham College, London and can be seen on the weathervane on The Royal Exchange in the City of London which was founded in 1565 by Gresham's nephew Sir Thomas Gresham. (There is a similar weathervane on The Faneuil Hall in Boston, Massachusetts which is modelled on The Royal Exchange.)

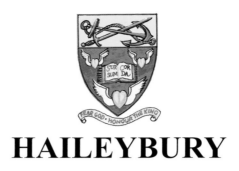

HAILEYBURY

Hubert Pragnell

Haileybury Quad

In 1806 The Honourable East India Company founded a college for the purpose of teaching and training future generations to govern British India. The site chosen for the college was an area of heathland in the Manor of Hailey near Hertford, twenty miles north of London. The architect chosen to build the new school was William Wilkins, who was later to design The National Gallery, Downing College Cambridge and much of The University of London. His buildings were in the Neo Classical style arranged round a large grass quadrangle, claimed to be the largest academic quadrangle in Europe. The College closed in 1858 after the collapse of The East India Company following the Indian Rebellion of 1857 and subsequent direct rule by the British Crown.

A speculator bought the existing buildings and the 500 acre estate and sold them for £18,000 to a group of local worthies who had in mind the founding of a Public School. The new School opened in 1862 and pupil numbers reached 500 by the middle of the 1870s. In 1877, a chapel was added, designed by the architect Arthur Blomfield, who also designed The Royal College of Music and Selwyn College, Cambridge. It was truly magnificent in design; its green Romanesque cupola totally dominating the school campus.

In 1874, a Haileybury Housemaster was appointed the first Headmaster of the United Services Proprietory College at Westward Ho! near Bideford in North Devon. In 1903 the College moved to Windsor and became the Imperial Service College (ISC). Rudyard Kipling wrote a fascinating account of his time at Westward Ho! in "*Stalkey & Co*". Two World Wars in quick succession dealt a massive blow to all schools associated with the military and Haileybury and ISC were hit harder than most. They merged in 1942 and the new school was officially renamed 'Haileybury and Imperial Service College'; now referred to as simply 'Haileybury'.

Since 1998, the School has been fully co-educational with a total population of 750 pupils of whom nearly 300 are girls and 500 are boarders.

Not surprisingly, several Old Boys have distinguished themselves in the Armed Services including Air Chief Marshal Sir Trafford Leigh- Mallory who was in charge of 12 Group Fighter Command during the Battle of Britain and was an advocate in the 'Big Wing' tactic. He was also Commander in Chief of the Allied Invasion of Normandy in 1943. He died in a plane crash over the French Alps in November 1944. Other distinguished Armed Services Alumni include Air Chief Marshal Sir Robert Brooke and two Marshals of the RAF Sir William Dickson (1954 – 58); and Sir John Slessor (1950 – 53). The army is represented by Field Marshals, Lord Allenby (Palestine Campaign 1917 – 18) and Sir John Chapple who was Chief of the General Staff from 1989 – 1992. The Royal Navy had a Haileyburian as First Sea Lord Admiral, Sir Jonathan Bond, who held this post from 2006 – 2009.

Away from the battlefield, other famous Haileyburians include the distinguished playwright, Alan Ayckbourn; businessman Lord Sainsbury and racing driver Stirling Moss.

IPSWICH SCHOOL

Clifford Bayly

School from Christchurch Park

In 1528 Cardinal Thomas Wolsey re-founded Ipswich School, his *alma mater*, as the Cardinal College of St Mary. At the same time he founded a university college of the same name at Oxford (later to become Christ Church). It was a twin foundation linking a school to a university in the same manner as Winchester College and New College Oxford (1382) and Eton and King's College Cambridge (1441).

Wolsey was born in 1475 at Ipswich, the son of a prosperous merchant, and after attending Ipswich School went on to Magdalen Hall, Oxford where he obtained his degree at the age of 15 and a fellowship a few years later. He was ordained priest at St Peter's Marlborough in 1498 and thus began a meteoric rise to power not matched since Becket.

The origins of Ipswich School go back to at least 1399, when it was connected with The Guild of Corpus Christi serving to educate the sons of its members. In 1483 Richard Felaw, MP for Ipswich, gave land and buildings for the accommodation and endowment of the School which at this time moved to Felaw's house. It was at about this time Wolsey became a pupil.

By the time Wolsey had re-founded the School in 1528 he had become Henry VIII's Lord Chancellor (equivalent to Prime Minister today); Archbishop of York, and, next to his monarch, the most powerful man in England. He settled a generous endowment on the School moving it to a site near St Peters Church where fine new buildings were erected.

It was to be the greatest school in England. However within two years he fell from grace, not only because of his legendary financial profligacy, but also because he could not secure Henry VIII's divorce from Queen Catherine. Wolsey was stripped of all of his assets and in 1530 Cardinal College was dissolved and the School returned to Felaw's House. All that remains of Wolsey's college today is its chapel, now called St Peter's Church and Wolsey's Gate, the watergate in College Street surmounted by the Royal arms of Henry VIII with the supporters reversed in error.

Henry VIII, however, did not abandon the School. In 1537 he re-endowed the masters' salaries, confirmed by his daughter, Queen Elizabeth I, who gave the School its Charter in 1566. For part of the School's history, it was known as 'Queen Elizabeth's Grammar School', Ipswich. The School's coat of arms are those Henry VIII as on Wolsey's Gate and the reigning monarch is the School's Visitor.

In 1614, the School crossed the road to occupy the former Refectory of the Blackfriars Priory abandoned since the Reformation. Here and in the former Dormitory the School remained for over 200 years until, in 1842, the buildings became unusable. In 1852 new buildings were erected in Henley Road opposite Christchurch Park. The Tudoresque red brick building designed by Architect Christopher Fleury, in a nod towards Wolsey, has a central tower which resembles Tom Tower at Christ Church, Oxford, founded by Wolsey as his Cardinal College of St Mary.

KIMBOLTON SCHOOL
Dennis Flanders

Kimbolton Castle

In terms of popular myth, Kimbolton School, founded in 1600, is forever associated with Kimbolton Castle, although in reality the School only took up residence in the castle in 1950 at which time it dropped the appellation 'Grammar' from its name. The co-founders of the School were two local tradesmen: Henry Bayle, a local fuller and William Dawson, a baker.

A Norman foundation, Kimbolton Castle's most famous inhabitant was a reluctant guest. King Henry VIII's first wife Catherine of Aragon was exiled there in 1534 and died two years later. Her host during this period was Sir Charles Wingfield, uncle of Edward Maria Wingfield.

Undoubtedly, Edward Maria Wingfield was the most illustrious owner of Kimbolton Castle. He was evicted from the Castle in 1600 as punishment for his part in the revolt against Queen Elizabeth I the previous year led by the Earl of Essex. However this proved a mere irritant to a man who was busy organising one of the greatest adventures of all time, the formation and promotion of 'The London Virginia Company'. Its expedition to Jamestown in 1607 was the first permanent settlement made by the English in the New World. Out of the 105 original settlers, Wingfield was at 57, by far the oldest. Crucially, he had alongside him the great adventurer, Captain John Smith, of Pocahontas fame. A formal declaration was made claiming Virginia for the Crown and Edward Wingfield was elected first President of the new Virginian colony (arguably America's first President). Had it not been for Wingfield's opportunism and organisation, Virginia might well have been colonised by the French or the Spanish.

During the early 17th century, whilst Wingfield was engaged in his New World adventures, Kimbolton Castle was sold to the Montagu Family who were to become successively Earls and Dukes of Manchester. The 2nd Earl commanded Parliament's Eastern Army in the early stages of The English Civil War (1642-1651), and is remembered as the castle's most illustrious owner. They made many improvements and in 1690 remodelled the castle to a design by Sir John Vanbrugh assisted by Nicholas Hawksmoor. At the same time the Venetian artist Pellegrini embellished the main staircase and state rooms with an outstanding set of murals. The Montagu family held the castle for 350 years until in 1950 the 10th Duke sold it to Kimbolton School. The 13th Duke now lives in California.

The Robert Adam Gatehouse has been adapted to school use and stands at the end of the wide High Street in the village of Kimbolton. There is also a fine display of fine portraits and other paintings by Lely and Mengs which still hang in the staterooms along with family portraits and the Pellegrini murals.

In his painting, Dennis Flanders was particularly proud of the effect that the splendid avenue of Wellingtonias had on the picture with their attendant shadows lying across the grass. The 'Wellingtonia (Sequoiadendron)' is the world's largest living thing and there are specimens more than 3000 years old in its native California. The ones at Kimbolton were planted in the 19th century.

THE KING'S SCHOOL, CANTERBURY

Dennis Flanders

Speech Day Garden Party

It is now generally accepted that King's Canterbury is the oldest school in Britain. The distinguished historian A.F. Leach, after exhaustive research and at first proclaiming St Peters York as the oldest, finally concluded that King's Canterbury was an even earlier foundation. He based this judgement on the fact that as each cathedral had within its precincts a school, then the oldest cathedral, Canterbury, must by definition, contain the oldest school. As church services were in Latin, it was necessary to teach the converts the Latin tongue; hence the need for a school. Therefore King's Canterbury can trace its origins back to c.597 when Augustine founded a cathedral at Canterbury.

King's owes its name to Henry VIII who, when he abolished St Augustine's Monastery at the time of the Reformation, re-endowed the School in 1541; continuity being maintained by reappointing the same Headmaster. At this time the same re-endowment process and change in nomenclature was taking place in other 'new' King's schools throughout England.

King's most influential Headmaster was F.J. Shirley who, during the period 1935-1962, transformed the School from a minor and nearly bankrupt institution into a truly great school. He had initiated extensive rebuilding, including a school hall deemed essential to any self respecting headmaster. Prior to his appointment, he had written to the Dean, Dr Hewlett Johnson, famous as the 'Red Dean', pointing out the deficiencies of the School. Despite what might have been perceived as temerity, he was appointed Headmaster. He made good the deficiencies and when he left twenty seven years later, finances were sound and numbers had increased from 200 to 500.

The King's School is inextricably entwined with the towering presence of the great Cathedral and its associated buildings. The Dark Entry passing Prior Selling's 15th century gateway was immortalized in Richard Barham's *"Ingoldsby Legends"*. The Norman Staircase leading up to the Old Schoolroom dates from 1150. Meister Omers house bears the name of a Dutchman who was in the service of the Priory from 1240 to 1280. In fact, until fairly recently, the main School buildings had always been within the Cathedral precincts. That is until 1976 when St Augustine's Abbey was acquired, situated outside the City walls.

Dennis Flanders' painting opposite, although somewhat dated, is a good example of the School's close physical identity with the Cathedral. It portrays the lively *va et vient* of a typical 1950s Speech Day Garden Party. It was part of a series of paintings which appeared in the Illustrated London News in 1959 under the title *"Great English Public Schools"*. The Dark Entry can be clearly seen to the left in the picture. Dr Shirley was no doubt most impressed, because he acquired the original painting which became part of the School's archives.

Distinguished alumni of King's include Christopher Marlowe, the Elizabethan dramatist; Thomas Linacre who entered the school in 1472 and in later life, founded The Royal College of Physicians; William Harvey who, in the 17th Century, discovered the circulation of the blood; and David Gower, England cricket captain.

THE KING'S SCHOOL, ELY

Dennis Flanders

The School Lane

King's School Ely is one of seven 'King's' Schools founded by Henry VIII in 1541 at the time of the Reformation. However some of these Schools like King's Ely had much earlier origins.

In 1970, a commemorative booklet was written by Rodney Saunders, then Head of the Junior School, celebrating the School's first thousand years. It was illustrated with pencil drawings by Dennis Flanders who, in 1992, produced the painting opposite. However a foundation date of 970 may be a somewhat modest claim as there seems to have been a school at Ely at a much earlier time.

The *"Liber Eilenis" (History of Ely)* written by a 12th century monk refers to the fact that people of the highest rank brought their children to be educated at the monastery founded by Queen Etheldreda in 673. She was the daughter of Anna, King of the East Angles, and an early convert to Christianity following Saint Augustine's arrival in Kent in 598. Etheldreda was the archetypal Anglo-Saxon woman; empowered, independent and wealthy. Twice divorced from husbands of arranged marriages, she used the dowry from her first marriage to found the monastery on the previously uninhabited Isle of Ely.

In 870, the monastery was destroyed by the Danish Vikings and was not rebuilt until 970 by Athelwold, Bishop of Winchester. A school became a concomitant of the monastic infrastructure, as was the usual practice. It is this later date which is officially claimed as its parturition. Edward the Confessor received the first part of his education at Ely before fleeing to Normandy with his parents, King Ethelred the Unready and Queen Emma. The deposed Ethelred's successor, Canute, the first Viking King of England, became a great benefactor to Ely; perhaps to expiate the destruction of Ely Abbey by his ancestors. In 1042, Edward, having returned to England and acceded to the throne, granted Ely a Charter confirming its rights and privilege. It gained full Cathedral status in 1109.

The School has always been closely associated with the Cathedral and since medieval times has had close connections with Cambridge University. Two colleges, Peterhouse (1269) and Jesus College (1496) were founded by Bishops of Ely. Some of the buildings used by the School, date from the medieval period. The Great Gateway of the Abbey called Ely Porta (14th century) is now used as the School's library. Other buildings dating from the 14th century are Prior Craudens Chapel used for smaller services and the monastic barn which is now the School's dining room. An earlier building is the 12th century Infirmary now used as the boarding house for the Ely Cathedral's boy choristers.

A feature which is unique to the school is The Hoop Trundle, which takes place near the east end of the Cathedral each year, to mark Henry VIII's designation of the school as a King's School in 1541. The event commemorates his declaration that Scholars, of which there are now twelve King's Scholars and twelve Queen's Scholars, should be allowed to trundle their hoops along the nave of the Cathedral in inclement weather.

LANCING COLLEGE

Dennis Flanders

Landscape

The painting opposite is of Lancing College Chapel viewed across the River Adur with the old wooden toll bridge in the foreground. Situated high up on the South Downs, it dominates the skyline in that part of Sussex just north of Shoreham. It is cathedral-like in proportion and splendour and rests on concrete piles 90 feet deep. Its interior is on the scale of the nave of Westminster Abbey. The Rose Window, at the West End, with its 30,000 pieces of glass, is the largest in any English church and was not finished until 1978. Beyond the cloistered Chapel two quadrangles, on a split level, nestle into the hillside. Their grey walls provide the largest area of finished flint in England.

Lancing College was founded in 1848 by Nathaniel Woodard, a curate at Shoreham. In his pamphlet *"A Plea for the Middle Classes"* Woodard had argued that an important and influential section of Victorian society; the newly emerging middle classes, were not properly provided for educationally. He called for more, less exclusive, Public Schools which would be imbued with his passion for Anglo-Catholicism (High Church). He had been greatly influenced by the tractarian credo of the Oxford Movement led by Newman, Keble and Pusey when an undergraduate at Oxford University.

In case his plea should fall on deaf ears, he got on with the job himself; bought two hundred and thirty acres on Lancing Hill and employed Richard Cromwell Carpenter as architect of the College who designed the earlier buildings. His son, Richard Herbert Carpenter designed the famous Chapel with William Slater.

Woodard was a fund raiser extraordinaire and his methods included pamphleteering, special events and huge public meetings with famous speakers. As a result, he became a national figure and friends with some of the richest men in England including two Prime Ministers. Prime Minister William Gladstone was a particular friend, and sites for his schools were donated by the Duke of Newcastle (Worksop) and Lord Brownlow (Ellesmere). When Woodard died in 1891 he had founded eleven schools. Today The Woodard Corporation now number thirty nine schools.

Probably Lancing's most famous alumnus is Evelyn Waugh, the author of *"Brideshead Revisited"*, who came here instead of Sherborne because his elder brother Alec, also a writer, had scandalised the Dorset school by writing the autobiographical *"The Loom of Youth"*

Lancing, now occupying a site of over 500 acres, is the flagship of The Woodard Corporation.

MALVERN COLLEGE

Jane Carpanini

Towards St George

On the 19ᵗʰ April 2009, the Morgan Motor Company celebrated its centenary by assembling around 150 Morgan cars of all vintages at Malvern College. It was in the engineering workshop at the College that the company's founder, Henry Morgan, built the first Morgan three wheeler. Working closely with him was the College's engineering master, William Stephenson Peach, grandson of the rail pioneer, George Stephenson. In 1901 Malvern had been one of the first schools to have an engineering workshop and Charles Morgan, grandson of the founder unveiled a plaque on its site, now the College's medical centre, to mark his company's Centenary.

In 1865 Malvern College was one of the spate of schools built in the Victorian era to satisfy the appetite of the newly enriched middle classes for educational establishments for their sons. The school was designed in the neo Gothic style by architect Charles Hansom who, a few years earlier, had designed Clifton College and Plymouth Cathedral, with his brother Joseph. (Joseph also designed the eponymous Hansom Cab). It was a proprietorial school with a share capital of £24,000 subscribed by local citizens.

Distinguished alumni of Malvern College include the novelist and scholar C.S. Lewis; actor Denholm Elliot, broadcaster and author Jeremy Paxman and interestingly the seven Foster brothers who all played cricket for Malvern and Worcestershire before the First World War.

Paramount amongst 'Fostershire' was R.E. (Tip) Foster who is the only man to have captained England at both football (1902) and cricket (1903). After Malvern, 'Tip' Foster attended University College, Oxford where he represented the University at cricket, football, racquets and golf. He captained Oxford at cricket and scored 930 runs at an average of 77.5 in the 1900 season; a record in University cricket. In the 1903 Ashes series at Sydney, in his first test match appearance for England, he scored 287 which was the highest score in test cricket until surpassed in 1930. (It still remains in 2011 the highest score by a debutant). In football, Foster played as a forward for the Corinthians and between 1900 and 1902 represented England five times, scoring a hat trick against Germany in 1901, and captaining his country against Wales in his final appearance. Tragically Foster died of diabetes in 1913 at the age of only 30.

In Jane Carpanini's painting, the College's setting beneath the Malvern Hills is brilliantly captured evoking images of Sir Edward Elgar and J.R.R. Tolkien who both gained inspiration from their beauty and grandeur.

MANCHESTER GRAMMAR SCHOOL

Dennis Roxby Bott

Main Drive and Archway

Hugh Oldham, the founder of Manchester Grammar School, is often rather snobbishly portrayed as being a not particularly intellectual prelate, probably because of his strong Lancashire accent. Born in 1452, he was appointed Bishop of Exeter in 1505 and founded Manchester Grammar School in 1515.

Oldham's formal education was impressive: he was a protégé of Lady Margaret Beaufort, the mother of Henry VII. She, after her fourth marriage to John Seymour, 1st Earl of Derby, had a ménage of promising young boys whose education she sponsored under the tutelage of an Oxford man, Thomas Westbury. Amongst the other pupils were the future Bishops of Lincoln and Ely, William Smyth and James Stanley.

What is particularly interesting is that, not only did Lady Margaret found two Cambridge Colleges: Christ's (1505) and St John's (1511) but her protégés were instrumental in founding two Oxford Colleges: Corpus Christi (Oldham 1517) and Brasenose (Smyth in 1509).

Oldham attended Exeter College, Oxford and Queen's College, Cambridge and then took Holy Orders. He received profitable livings from his schoolboy chum, William Smyth when the latter became Bishop of Lincoln. However his great wealth came from his water powered corn and malt mills on the River Irk in Manchester, which were to fund Manchester Grammar School for over 200 years.

He was a born entrepreneur and a shrewd politician who foresaw the coming changes of The Reformation. He persuaded his friend, Richard Fox, to found an Oxford College, Corpus Christi, rather than a monastery. What is more, it was to be a secular college and the finest in Oxbridge for teaching the Classics. He even contributed a massive £4,000 to assist its foundation.

In 1516 Oldham acquired Long Millgate, a piece of land on the River Irk, and built Manchester Grammar School which was opened in 1518. This building was replaced in 1776 on the same site and in 1870 a further new building was added, designed by Alfred Waterhouse.

In 1930, after over 400 years in the city centre, the School moved to more spacious surroundings in Old Hall Lane, Fallowfield, just over three miles away. The new main building was designed, Oxbridge style, with a quadrangle by Francis Jones and Percy Worthington and is approached from Old Hall Lane by a long tree lined drive or avenue.

Interestingly, the coats of arms of both Manchester Grammar School and Corpus Christi both contain a rebus on Oldham's name in the form of three owls. This suggests that he pronounced his name in the local accent as 'Owldem'. Owls are also to be seen in the coat of arms of the Borough of Oldham. He never bothered to refine his Lancashire accent.

MARLBOROUGH COLLEGE

Jane Carpanini

Court

Marlborough College stands on the site of a Neolithic monument which is over 4500 years old. The mound that rises among its buildings is as old as its near neighbour Silbury though, at 60 feet, is only half as high. Of chalk construction it is, after Silbury, the second biggest man made mound in Europe.

William the Conqueror built one of his castles here because it was on the route to all points westward from London. It was much frequented by monarchs in the 12th and 13th centuries but during the 14th century fell into ruin. However it remained in royal hands until 1536 when Henry VIII, having married Jane Seymour, gifted it to her brother Edward the 1st Duke of Somerset. A house was built on the site at this time which was replaced in 1711 by a grand mansion. With the death of the 7th Duke of Somerset in 1750, the mansion was leased out and turned into a fashionable coaching inn. The Castle Inn did a roaring trade catering for the gentry on their way from London to Bath. Distinguished visitors included two prime ministers: William Pitt (Lord Chatham) and the Duke of Wellington. The advent of the railways in the 1840s led to the rapid demise of the coaching business and with it The Castle Inn.

In 1843, a group of Church of England clergymen with the backing of the Archbishop of Canterbury were looking to establish a boarding school to educate the sons of the clergy. They took a lease on the now vacant Castle Inn and Marlborough College was opened in August 1843 with the admission of 199 boys.

A chapel was hastily built in 1848, but it proved to be inadequate both aesthetically and in size, as, by 1880, pupil numbers had reached 600; so it was even more hastily demolished. A new and much grander chapel was built occupying a dominant position at the entrance to the Court. Designed by Bodley and Garner, it contains a treasure house of artistic artefacts, including murals by Spencer Stanhope; a sculpture by Alan Durst and stained glass from Edward Burne-Jones and William Morris.

William Morris had been a pupil at Marlborough when, in 1851, he played a leading part in the infamous rebellion by pupils against the harsh and Spartan regime then operating at the College. The Master left and so did Morris along with many others. A new Master, George Cotton, was appointed. He came from Rugby and was a disciple of the legendary Thomas Arnold, Headmaster of Rugby who was the epitome of enlightened education. In his six years as Master, he got the School under control and set it on the path to future success. He left to become Bishop of Calcutta where he set up many fine schools.

Distinguished literary alumni include two poets who refer to their alma mater in their writings, Siegfried Sassoon in *"The Old Century"* and John Betjemen in *"Summoned by Bells"*.

METHODIST COLLEGE, BELFAST

Grahame Booth

School House

In 1865, when Methodists in Ireland numbered only 23,000 out of a total population of six million, it was decided to build a college in Belfast, partly for the training of Methodist ministers and partly as a school for boys. Money was collected, mainly from the Irish Methodists but with help from England and America, and 15 acres of land were acquired on what were then the very outskirts of the city. The foundation stone of the 'New Wesleyan College' at Belfast (as it was originally known) was laid on 28th August 1865 by Sir William McArthur, a Londonderry businessman, who later became Lord Mayor of London.

Three years later, on 18th August 1868, the College was opened with 141 pupils. Shortly after the opening a proposal that 'young ladies' be educated on equal terms with the boys was accepted by the committee of Management, with the result that, from the third month of its existence, Methodist College has been a co-educational establishment.

In 1891, Sir William McArthur bequeathed a large sum of money towards the foundation of the hall of residence for girl boarders. The College steadily flourished and the enrolment increased. There was a rapid growth of numbers after 1920, when the theological department moved to Edgehill College thus releasing more accommodation for the college's use.

Methodist College has continued to grow, with each decade seeing new developments and initiatives. The extensive grounds of Pirrie Park were acquired in 1932, and Downey House, one of two Houses in the Preparatory Department,

was opened shortly afterwards. The Whitla Hall, built with a bequest from Sir William Whitla, was opened in December 1935.

With the outbreak of World War II, Belfast was subject to heavy bombing but the College continued to function as normal. Girl boarders moved into School House with the boys, and the McArthur and Whitla Halls were used as refuge centres for people bombed out of their homes. The College even acquired a fire engine and the staff were trained as air raid wardens, keeping nightly vigils in case of further enemy attacks.

In 1950, Fullerton House was established as a Preparatory Department on the Malone Road Campus. A major rebuilding scheme in the same decade included the construction of new science laboratories. In 1992, a suite of Science and Technology Rooms was added, to commemorate the award of the Nobel Prize to former pupil, Ernest Walton, honoured for his work on splitting the atom.

In celebration of the College's Centenary, a large sum of money was raised to build the Chapel of Unity, a place of peace and reflection, open to all members of the College community. It houses a magnificent pipe organ, a gift from Corpus Christi College, Cambridge and in the outer oak doors is carved the College motto: "Deus Nobiscum, God Is With Us". This reflects the Christian values that remain at the heart of the work of Methodist College.

MILLFIELD SCHOOL

John Newberry

View from the South

The circumstances surrounding the foundation of Millfield School are the most bizarre and unlikely of any leading Independent School in the British Isles. The key players in Millfield's birth in 1935 were Jack Meyer (1905-1991), an English cotton broker in Bombay and an Indian Maharaja who wished to set up a small school in England to educate his princely sons.

Jack Meyer had a distinguished academic and sporting education at Haileybury and Cambridge where he represented the University at four separate sports. After graduating in 1926, the Haileybury connection with its Imperial College imprimatur (see page 68) helped him secure a job with a cotton broking firm in Bombay.

In 1929 Jack Meyer realised that cotton broking was not for him so he accepted a teaching post at one of the state schools run by his sporting friend, the England Test cricketer, Prince Ranjit Singh. Three years later, having realised that his true vocation was teaching, he secured a post with the Maharaja of Dhrangadhre to oversee his Palace School.

Then in 1935, the Maharaja decided that his three sons should have an English education with Jack Meyer as their tutor. Three more local princes' sons were added plus The First Minister's son and the whole entourage moved to England. A large house called Mill Field was found in Street, Somerset, owned by the Clark family whose eponymous shoe manufacturing company was situated in the town. In this unlikely location Millfield School was established within sight of Glastonbury Tor.

Jack Meyer's unique teaching methods, based on small class sizes and intensive small group coaching, produced remarkable results particularly in the case of children with learning difficulties. In 1941 the dyslexic son of Clement Atlee, then the Deputy Prime Minister, was sent to Millfield and received crucial help and coaching which enabled him to pass his entrance exams to the School of Navigation at Southampton. Word started to spread at government and society level about a school in the West Country where young people with severe reading problems could be helped. This really put Millfield on the map and, by the time he retired in 1971, Jack Meyer had purchased the freehold of the building from the Clark family.

Apart from its undoubted academic achievements, Millfield has always encouraged sporting excellence by awarding sporting scholarships to those boys and girls with exceptional talent. Among those who have benefitted are Gareth Edwards, the Welsh Rugby International.

However, the most distinguished Millfield sporting alumnus is Mary Rand M.B.E. (nee Bignall). At the 1964 Olympic Games in Tokyo she won a gold medal in the long jump; a silver medal in the pentathlon; and a bronze medal in the 4 x 100metres relay.

MONMOUTH SCHOOL

Clifford Bayly

School House from River Wye

Monmouth School, established in 1614, is yet another example of a school administered by a City Livery Company on behalf of a native livery man who made good.

William Jones was a native of Monmouth who features in Thomas Fuller's *"The History of the Worthies of England"*(1665). He is described as escaping to London to avoid his creditors where he first became a porter and then, by his brains, a factor, travelling to Hamburg to sell Welsh wool. Such was his success, that, by 1600, he was invited to become a member of the livery of The Worshipful Company of Haberdashers.

William Jones died childless and by his Will left over half his fortune to charity including £9,000 to the Haberdashers for the sole purpose of establishing a free school and alms house in the town of Monmouth and Newland. Importantly, he specified that a preacher should be ordained to lecture at the two new institutions. He had extremely puritanical views reflecting the mood of the time which was very much anti- popery. He was eager to evangelise the Marches of Wales where recusancy was still strong.

In 1542, Monmouthshire had been annexed to England by virtue of it becoming part of Oxford Assizes. During the Civil War of 1642 – 1651 Monmouth changed hands three times between Charles I Royalists and Cromwell's Commonwealth forces who destroyed Monmouth Castle. Monmouth remained in England until 1972 when the Local Government Act confirmed that Monmouth's place was in Wales.

The English Civil War (1642-1651) and its consequent financial demands on Livery Companies meant that money was in short supply, and the School suffered as a result. Another continuing problem was the antagonism between Town Authorities and the Haberdashers in London over the running of the School. The selection of Headmasters, Ushers and Lecturers (Preacher) was always being disputed. Numbers dropped to only three by the mid-18th century.

Before moving on from this period, it is interesting to note that in 1669 the 1st Duke of Monmouth was created by Charles II. He was the King's illegitimate son by Lucy Walter and was greatly favoured by his father. However he ended up on the gallows having fiercely opposed his father's successor James II.

The fortunes of the Haberdashers greatly improved in the mid-19th century due to wise investment in the New Cross area. As a result, Monmouth School was completely rebuilt between 1864 –1878, by architect William Snooke. School House with its ceremonial entrance facing Wye Bridge was added by Henry Stock in 1895.

The New Cross effect also meant that a girls' school could be opened in 1892 at Hardwick House and then in 1897 a new landmark site was found on the Hereford Road above the town.

The two schools have flourished in the last 100 years and often have combined activities, particularly theatre productions at the new Blake Theatre; there is some co-educational teaching in the sixth form.

NORWICH SCHOOL

Dennis Roxby Bott

The View towards Erpingham Gate

The See of East Anglia was first established by St Felix, Bishop of the East Angles, at Dunwich in 630. It was then moved to Elham in 637; Thetford in 1075 and finally to Norwich in 1094 by Bishop Herbert de Losinga.

As was customary with the establishment of any cathedral, a grammar school for the teaching of Latin was also established. So, in 1096, the origins of Norwich School can be found with the establishment by Bishop de Losinga of an Episcopal Grammar School. The first recorded headmaster was Vincent de Scarning in 1250.

In 1285, a second school was founded, known as 'The Amonry School'. This was merged with The Episcopal School in 1516. In 1540, after the Reformation, the School became known as 'King Henry VIII's Grammar School'.

However in 1547, Henry's son Edward re-founded the School as 'King Edward's VI's Grammar School' under the Great Hospital Charter. It was separated from the Cathedral foundation and placed under the control of the Mayor and Alderman of Norwich. This move was a demonstration of Edward VI's fervent desire to remove all traces of Popery along with his suppression of Chantries. In 1551 the School moved into its current buildings; School House and the School Chapel; the former College and Chantry of St John the Evangelist which had been dissolved in 1547.

However, Norwich School remains inextricably linked to the Cathedral; as well as supplying and educating the trebles in the Cathedral Choir, members of the Senior School have the privilege of meeting in the Cathedral every morning. Norwich Cathedral is unusual in many ways, not only does it possess the oldest Bishop's throne in use in any English Cathedral, it also, like Ely and Salisbury, does not have a ring of bells. Its spire at 315 feet is the second tallest in England (only the spire of Salisbury Cathedral is higher at 404 feet).

Norwich School's most distinguished alumnus is Viscount Horatio Nelson who was born at Burnham Thorpe Rectory.

Dennis Roxby Bott, in the view opposite, has painted a scene he knows well, having trained at the prestigious Norwich School of Art whose provenance can be traced back to the Norwich Society of Artists who were hugely influential in the development of European landscape painting in the 19th century. John Sell Cotman and Alfred Munnings were leading adherents; the former being a Norvicensian.

OUNDLE SCHOOL

Ken Howard

The View from the Great Hall

The small market town of Oundle which is pre-Conquest is totally dominated by Oundle School which is now the third largest Independent School in Great Britain with over 1,000 pupils. Only Eton and Millfield are larger. Its teeming vitality in term time is in contrast to the somnolent serenity during the long vacations.

Oundle School owes its unique place in academic folklore to one man, Frederick Sanderson, who, with Thomas Arnold at Rugby and Edward Thring at Uppingham, was one of the seminal influences on educational methods and practice in the 19th and early 20th centuries. In his thirty years as Headmaster (1892 -1922), he transformed Oundle School into one of Britain's leading Independent Schools.

Oundle has not always been a great school. Known to exist in 1485, it was in 1556 re-endowed by a legacy from a former pupil, Sir William Laxton. The medium for his munificence was 'The Worshipful Company of Grocers' of which he had been Master as well as being Lord Mayor of London. Over 450 years later, the School is still governed by 'The Worshipful Company of Grocers'.

The School fell on hard times and by the 1890s was in terminal decline. In 1892, in a moment of divine *afflatus* or maybe desperation, the Governors appointed Frederick Sanderson as Headmaster. In a period when a classical education was the usual prerequisite for headmasters of Public Schools, his non-Public School background and a degree in Maths and Physics, (albeit a first class from Durham), made him a most unlikely choice. Moreover, he was not even an athlete. However he had been an Assistant Master at Dulwich where he had transformed the teaching of Science and Engineering

Education in the vibrant Victorian era was out of touch with the needs of the age. Before Sanderson's time Science had been regarded as of interest to only a minority of specialists. He saw to it that every boy spent time working in the Science and Engineering laboratories which he set up. Dynamos, heat engines, motors, a forge, a foundry and even a meteorological station appeared in a scholastic revolution. It was arranged for each form to spend a week in the workshops every term. Oundle was years ahead of any other school. The Engineering legacy survives into the 21st century with boys and girls renovating cars and building off-road buggies to an Oundle School design.

Oundle's sporting legacy is also impressive. The Rugby XV has a particularly high reputation. Old Oundelians can boast 28 Blues at Oxbridge and twelve international honours. In cricket there is a unique achievement: both father Michael Mills and son Peter captained Cambridge University in 1948 and 1982 respectively.

Ken Howard's painting shows the Gate Tower entrance to the Cloister and Quad, the hub of the School, designed by Arthur Blomfield in the late 19th century. This composition from beside the Great Hall is a favourite view for artists as it captures the lively *'va et vient'* of the School.

PORTORA ROYAL SCHOOL

Grahame Booth

View from the River Erne

In 1608 five Royal Schools were established in Ulster by the Royal Proclamation of James I. These were to be situated in the counties of Armagh, Cavan, Donegal, Fermanagh and Tyrone. Their purpose was to provide a Protestant education for the children of immigrants from Scotland and England in furtherance of the English Government's policy of Plantation. This policy was designed to ensure Protestant domination in the north of Ireland. First of all large areas were confiscated from three principal land owners in Ulster: the Earls O'Neil, O'Donnel and O'Doherty, all Catholics and all thought to be against the Government. Their plight is described in history as the "Flight of the Earls" as they fled to the continent and settled in Rome where they died in exile. Their lands were seized and redistributed to the immigrants from Scotland and England. Trinity College, Dublin and the Anglican Church of Ireland were also beneficiaries of this land redistribution.

The Plantation policy was overseen by Sir Arthur Chichester, Lord Deputy of Ireland, and it was he who decided that the Enniskillen island site should be the County Town of Fermanagh. However, Fermanagh's first school was located at Ballybalfour, 10 miles south of Enniskillen, which had been built by Sir James Balfour, a prominent Scottish settler who also fully funded the new school. The School only lasted 30 years at Ballybalfour before political pressure had it moved, in 1648, to Schoolhouse Lane in the new town of Enniskillen. Of the five Royal Schools, Fermanagh enjoyed the wealthiest foundation and largest endowments.

In 1763, Revd Mark Noble became the eighth Master of the School and found a school that was dingy, cramped and lacking in facilities. So much so, that pupil numbers had dropped to only 24. Noble found a superb 33 acre site on Portora Hill, just outside Enniskillen town centre, and spent nearly £ 3,000 of his own money to complete the new school which was opened in 1779. The result was most gratifying because the school's geographical location on Portora Hill overlooking the River Erne was stunning. The 'School on the Hill' flourished and its Mastership became one of the most prestigious appointments in academic circles in Ireland. It has always been well connected to Trinity College, Dublin and the established Church of Ireland but it has never discriminated on religious grounds in its intake of pupils. Interestingly, Trinity College, Dublin has, over the 400 years, provided 22 Masters at Portora.

Until 1857 the school had been known as 'Enniskillen Royal School' but the Revd William Steele instigated the change of name to 'Portora Royal School' which was a sobriquet the locals had been using for some years. During Steele's time (1857 – 1891) Portora became the social Eton of Ireland.

Distinguished alumni include two icons of literature whose blue plaques adorn the front of the main school buildings: Oscar Wilde, a pupil between 1864 -1871 and Samuel Beckett, a pupil between 1920-1923.

RADLEY COLLEGE

Jane Carpanini

Mansion and Chapel

St Peter's College Radley was founded in 1847 by William Sewell and Robert Corbet Singleton. Sewell had formerly been Professor of Moral Philosophy at Oxford University. The school is located on elevated ground seven miles south of Oxford in a park of some six hundred acres. In this setting stands the beautiful 18th century mansion which Sewell and Singleton originally leased to house the whole school. The Mansion was built in 1720 for Sir John Stonehouse by William Townesend the leading Master Mason in Oxford, who was part of the Townesend dynasty of architects who worked in Oxford between1648-1800. They seemed to have worked on most of the College buildings at one time or another. The park was landscaped by Capability Brown in 1770. Sewell and Singleton considered that beautiful surroundings were beneficial to a boy's well-being as was the provision of an education on the principles of the Church of England.

The first bespoke buildings were a bell tower; a chapel; and a dormitory with separate cubicles and strict rules of silence at night. The new chapel was built in 1895 by Sir Thomas Jackson who was, between 1876 and 1914, responsible for more buildings in Oxford than any other architect of any period, including the Examination Schools and the Bridge of Sighs.

There are over six hundred and eighty pupils in the school who enter one of the ten houses known as 'Socials'. Because Sewell was an Oxford don he copied some university features. The boys still wear black gowns and the masters are known as 'dons'. Radley is one of the few remaining Independent schools that is all boys and all boarding.

The Charities Act 2006 highlighted the requirement for charities to demonstrate that they provide a public benefit or risk losing their charitable status. However in the case of Radley, public benefit has always been part of its ethos. The College has for decades made its facilities available, not only to the local community, but also further afield. Since 1994 annual trips have been organised to help underprivileged children from Romania. Radleians help at local primary schools and these schools also use Radley's facilities. However its sporting facilities are the most significant contribution. Its Cricket Academy, open to local schools and district cricket at no cost, has a county-wide reputation and Andrew Strauss, the England Cricket Captain, is an Old Radleian. Radley's swimming pool, athletics track and gymnasium are all used by local clubs and other schools.

In 2008 the building of a real tennis court was completed at Radley with former World Champion, Chris Ronaldson, becoming the resident professional. There are now four schools in Britain possessing real tennis courts. Out of a total of forty-five courts worldwide, twenty-six are situated in Britain. Real tennis was the forerunner of all racket sports and is thought to have originated in Tuscany in about the 5th century AD. Henry V played but it was Henry VIII who popularised the game in England and built a court at Hampton Court in 1530. At this time there were about 200 courts in Paris alone and by the early 17th century there were 14 courts in London. Real tennis declined in popularity from about 1700, although it has seen a revival since 1970. Radley is the only school in Britain possessing its own facilities for all the racket sports.

REPTON SCHOOL

Dennis Roxby Bott

Old Priory through the Arch

Repton is a small town situated 8 miles south of Derby on the south bank of the River Trent. In Anglo Saxon times it was of great importance, being at one time the capital of Mercia, and two Mercian Kings, Ethelbald and Wiglaf, are said to have been buried here. St Wystan, the grandson of King Wiglaf, was brutally murdered in AD 849 and his subsequent martyrdom caused the crypt at Repton to become an important place of pilgrimage. The Anglo Saxon church was neglected by the Danish Vikings and lay in ruins for over 100 years before being restored in AD 920. Its 212ft spire, added in 1340, is a landmark for miles around.

A priory was founded alongside St Wystans Church in about 1172 but was dissolved in 1538 during The Reformation. Much of the Priory was deliberately destroyed by the Thacker family into whose ownership it had passed. Fortunately what remained of the Priory was purchased by the Executors of Sir John Port in 1557 in order to found a school at Repton in furtherance of instructions contained in his Will. What remained was the Undercroft, the Prior's Chambers and Guest Hall which viewed through the Priory Arch is the enduring image of Repton School today and the subject of Dennis Roxby Bott's painting opposite.

In the early 17th century there were as many as 300 pupils at Repton but by 1800 there was only one. This decline was typical for Public Schools during the 18th century and was caused by religious and academic turpitude at the time. However, the arrival of Dr Steuart Adolphus Pears as Headmaster in 1854 heralded the 'second founding' of the School. He undertook a massive programme of improvements including building the School Chapel and Orchard House plus greatly expanding boarding and classroom accommodation. He positioned the School ideally so that it could take advantage of the mid-Victorian appetite for education. As a consequence Repton became a leading Public School.

Another Pears' legacy was his belief that sport was conducive to a healthy mind. This environment produced the legendary C.B. Fry who is best known for his cricketing prowess and is one of nine Reptonians who have represented England at cricket. Fry also obtained Blues at Oxford for football and athletics and even broke the world long jump record in his first varsity match. Other sporting alumni include Harold Abrahams, Olympic 100yds gold medallist in 1924; and tennis legend, Bunny Austin, a twice beaten finalist at Wimbledon in 1932 and 1938.

Repton has close associations with three successive Archbishops of Canterbury: William Temple, Geoffrey Fisher and Michael Ramsey. The first two were both Headmasters and the latter a pupil at Repton. Perhaps not so surprising because it is claimed that Christianity was first preached in the Midlands (Mercia) at the recently restored Market Cross in the centre of Repton.

In 2006, Repton launched an international boarding school in Dubai. This was a first and will enable pupil exchanges to be a feature of the Repton curriculum and thus prepare young people for the global market place of the future.

ROEDEAN SCHOOL

Jane Carpanini

School Landscape

Roedean School is one of Britain's most prestigious Independent girls' Schools. It has a splendid position above the cliffs overlooking the sea between Brighton and Rottingdean. On its chalky eyrie the School is buffeted by the prevailing south westerly winds which have undoubtedly contributed to the image of Roedean girls as being tough and hardy.

The School was founded in 1885 as 'Wimbledon House School' at 25, Lewes Crescent, in Kemp Town. The founders were three remarkable sisters; Penelope, Dorothy and Millicent Lawrence. They were, in effect, joint principals although Penelope was the driving force. She had studied the Sciences at Newnham College, Cambridge, passing the National Science Tripos, but did not receive a degree because women were denied degrees at Cambridge until 1947.

The School quickly outgrew the buildings in Lewes Crescent and Penelope Lawrence was able to acquire land from the Marquis of Abergavenny, in an area to the east of Brighton known as 'Roedean', on which to build a new school.

In 1898, the School moved to its new home, whose buildings were designed by the architect, John William Simpson, who, in 1919, became President of the Royal Institute of British Architects.

Impressive though the buildings were they had a slightly forbidding appearance and were dubbed 'Colditz on Sea' by later pupils. However in 2008, the School was given a facelift: a lime wash makeover which gives it a softer buttermilk and honey image.

Roedean has a sister School in Johannesburg, South Africa founded in 1903 by the youngest Lawrence sister, Theresa, with her friend Katherine Earle. Both girls were educated at Newnham College Cambridge.

Interestingly for a girls' school, Roedean has an impressive list of 'Old Boys' who were stationed at Roedean during the Second World War. In 1940 the girls were evacuated to the Keswick Hotel in the Lake District and, almost immediately, the Royal Navy requisitioned Roedean School which became 'HMS Vernon'; a shore based training establishment. During the war some 31,500 officers and men passed through the school on various courses. The young sailors particularly liked the bell push above every student's bed which had a notice below with the legend "Press the button if you need a mistress!"

Jane Carpanini's painting captures the ethos and sense of place that is uniquely Roedean.

ROYAL GRAMMAR SCHOOL
NEWCASTLE UPON TYNE
Dennis Roxby Bott

Eskdale Terrace Front

Unlike most early schools in Britain, Newcastle's first grammar school did not have an ecclesiastical origin. It was quite unusual in being founded by a local authority: The Mayor and Burgesses of Newcastle upon Tyne. By the terms of his Will, made in 1525, the Mayor Thomas Horsley made provision for the part payment of the salary of a grammar school master. On his death in 1545, the town's authorities agreed to supplement Horsley's endowment with a further 4 marks (£2.67) per annum and a school was set up in the grounds of St Nicholas Church. In about 1585, the school moved to the Hospital of St Mary the Virgin in Westgate. This was no ordinary hospital because it was controlled by the Mayor and Burgesses and was the place where the Town's Guild had met since the 14th century and remained the place where the Mayor and Council met until 1844.

This unusual connection between the Hospital and the Civic Authorities arose as a result of Newcastle's uniquely secular development. It was a mercantile town. From the 13th century onwards Newcastle prospered as a port and a centre for coal mining. It had very few ecclesiastical institutions; only four churches and, until 1882, no cathedral. Therefore the Burgesses took control of all religious and charitable institutions including the Hospital. As a result, the Hospital became the home of the Royal Grammar School until 1844 when it was demolished to make way for the new Central Station.

In 1600 Queen Elizabeth granted the Charter to formally found the Grammar School which for a while bore her name until it became known simply as the 'Royal Grammar School' (RGS). The Civic Authorities had provided bursaries for its boys to attend Oxford and Cambridge Universities since the 16th century and in the 17th century 143 boys went to the Universities (mostly Cambridge). At this time RGS was one of the great nurseries of the Northern elite due mainly to Hugh Moises, who was Headmaster between 1749-1787. He was so eminent a man that, at a time when education was generally on the decline in England, he raised the reputation at RGS to the highest level. There is a monument to Hugh Moises in the Cathedral and a memorial to a former pupil, Admiral Lord Colingwood, Nelson's second-in-command at Trafalgar. Another alumnus is Nicholas Ridley, Bishop of London who was one of the Oxford Martyrs burnt in 1555.

After the demolition of the School in 1844, the Council relocated it to temporary premises in the city centre before a new school was built at Rye Hill in 1870. However because of its city centre location, there was no space for sports pitches and it did not attract pupils from the prosperous northern suburbs. Therefore in 1905 the School moved to Jesmond on the northern edge of the city a few minutes walk from the Haymarket. RGS has prospered in its new location in Eskdale Terrace particularly as the Jesmond station of the famous Tyneside Metro is right outside.

RUGBY SCHOOL

Dennis Roxby Bott

View from the Close

At the end of the 18th century, Rugby, like most Public Schools in England, was lacking in proper organisation. There were no organised games and pupils spent their leisure time fighting, drinking, racing and poaching. Discipline was maintained by frequent beatings. As a result in 1797, under a particularly severe Headmaster Henry ('Black Tiger') Ingles, a pupils' rebellion took place, no doubt inspired by the French Revolution. The 'Riot Act' was read by William Butlin, a local Justice of the Peace and the local Militia were called in to break up the rebellion. The leading protagonists were savagely beaten or expelled.

Against this background, a saviour arrived who was to be a seminal influence on English Public School education. Dr Thomas Arnold was appointed Headmaster of Rugby in 1828 and introduced his brand of muscular Christianity which put an end to the severe conditions that had previously prevailed. He increased the powers of the Prefects who were to act in concert with the Headmaster and, most importantly, introduced the House System. Housemasters were given independence with a special emphasis on pastoral care. Organised games were gradually introduced by the boys and dubious outside activities were banned. His declared objective was the creation of Christian Gentlemen. Arnold's pupils became Headmasters of at least fourteen other schools, so his influence quickly spread. Sadly in 1842 he was cut down in his prime when he died at the age of only 47.

Life during Dr Arnold's time is recorded for posterity in Thomas Hughes' classical book *" Tom Brown's Schooldays"*. Hughes attended Rugby between 1834 – 1842.

In 1823, the pre Arnold period, when games were not subject to proper control or codified rules, William Webb Ellis caught the football and ran with it in his arms and thus Rugby Football was born. It was fitting that in 1845 the first rules of Rugby Football were formulated at Rugby School. Pilgrims come to pay homage at the Webb Ellis Rugby Football Museum now housed in the town centre in a building where the shoe and boot maker, James Gilbert, first made rugby boots in 1842.

Another factor in Rugby School's success is an auspicious foundation made by Lawrence Sheriff, a freeman of 'The Grocers Company' who like many a local lad made his fortune in London and founded a school in his native town. Sheriff endowed Rugby in his Will of 1567 (the year he died) which later included a codicil adding land in Middlesex which included an area which later became Conduit Street, Mayfair, which proved to be a very valuable windfall.

Architecturally, the School contains many buildings designed by the iconic William Butterfield who designed Keble College, Oxford. Old Big School and The Temple Reading Room are some of his designs; the latter named after another famous Head Master, Dr Frederick Temple, who reigned at Rugby from 1858–1869 and went on to become Archbishop of Canterbury. Butterfield's crowning glory at the School is the Chapel of 1872 beneath which lies the body of Thomas Arnold.

ST ALBANS SCHOOL

Dennis Roxby Bott

Abbey Gateway

From its foundation by Abbot Wulsin in 948, St Albans was for nearly six hundred years, the Abbey School. It grew up in close association with the great monastery established by King Offa in the 8th century around the shrine of St Alban, the first English martyr (c.264).

The early School was situated on Romeland Hill just north of the Abbey's 'Great Gateway' which was built in 1361 and now belongs to the School, having been purchased by the Governors in 1871. After the dissolution of the Monastery in 1539, the Great Gateway was for over three hundred years used as a prison. In fact, during the Napoleonic Wars, it housed French prisoners of war.

The School must have been flourishing by the end of the 11th century because the Abbot of St Albans, Richard Davlerney, summoned from France a learned layman, Geoffrey de Gorham, to become Master. Unfortunately, the journey from France was protracted and by the time he arrived a replacement had been appointed. Undeterred, Geoffrey de Gorham first took up another teaching appointment at Dunstable before becoming a monk in St Albans Abbey and rising to become Abbot in 1119. This story illustrates the fact that St Albans was clearly at this time a school of some importance.

After the closure of the Monastery in 1539, the last Abbot, Geoffrey de Gorham, purchased the Lady Chapel of the Abbey Church for £100 for the use of the School, but it was not until 1570 in the reign of Elizabeth I that the School's re-foundation was put on a firm footing. In that year, Sir Nicholas Bacon (father of Sir Francis Bacon) was instrumental in obtaining the famous Wine Charter from Queen Elizabeth. This allowed the School to receive a proportion of the profits from the sale of the wine within the Borough of St Albans. This very lucrative source of revenue continued until 1922 when it was commuted into a capital payment of £1,200 in full and final settlement.

As in many great schools throughout history, certain headmasters have had a seminal influence. The re-foundation of the School after The Reformation is generally acknowledged as being in 1570, soon after which, John 'Hylocomius' Thomas was appointed Master. A refugee from the Low Countries, he was a man who established a reputation internationally as a scholar and educationalist. In his twenty-six years as Master, he set the School on the path of stability and educational excellence.

Since the 19th century there have been many additions to the School site which now comprises a very eclectic mixture of architectural styles with buildings dating from the 14th century.

The claim to be St Albans' most illustrious alumnus must be a choice between Nicholas Breakspear, afterwards Pope Adrian IV, the only English Pope (1154 – 59) who famously granted Ireland to the English King Henry II, and, at the other historical extreme, Professor Stephen Hawking, the world-famous astrophysicist.

ST EDWARD'S, OXFORD

Ken Howard

Apsley, The Chapel Cloister and Library.

St Edward's was founded in 1863 at New Inn, Hall Street in Central Oxford, by the Revd Thomas Chamberlain, a passionate supporter of the Anglo Catholic Oxford Movement led by Keble, Newman and Pusey.

In 1873, the School's second headmaster, the Revd A.B. Simeon moved the School to its present 110 acre site in the Woodstock Road, adjacent to the suburb of Summertown. He immediately commissioned a local architect, William Wilkinson, who had already designed the Randolph Hotel, to commence the main school buildings. These were Gothic style red brick with a stone chapel. The quadrangle is the second largest in Oxford after Christ Church.

The School is named after the Anglo Saxon King, Edward II, great grandson of King Alfred. He came to the throne in AD 972 at the age of 13. Three years later he was murdered at the instigation of his step mother in order that her natural son, Ethelred should inherit the throne. On the steps of Corfe Castle he was stabbed with a dagger while drinking from a loving cup given by his step mother. The reason for naming the school after St Edward, King and martyr, is not clear; but his memory is kept alive in the School's cup and dagger emblem.

St Edward's alumni have a particularly distinguished record in the Second World War (1939-45). The RAF heroes, Group Captain Douglas Bader; Wing Commander Guy Gibson; Wing Commander Adrian Warburton; Sergeant Pilot Arthur Banks and Wing Commander Louis Strange were all former pupils. The exploits of the legless pilot Douglas Bader and Guy Gibson who was awarded the Victoria Cross for leading the raid on the Möhne and Eder dams have been well documented in major feature films *"Reach for the Sky"* and *"The Dambusters"*. However the deeds of the three other RAF heroes are just as amazing.

Louis Strange (1891 – 1966) served as an airman in both World Wars. He was awarded a DFC and the Military Cross in 1915 for carrying out one of the first tactical bombing missions. In 1940, aged 49, he returned as a Pilot Officer in the RAF Volunteer Reserve. He was soon on active service in France where he was awarded a bar to his DFC. Adrian Warburton was described by Air Chief Marshal, Arthur Tedder, as the most valuable pilot in the RAF. He was fearless and unorthodox and his speciality was low level photo reconnaissance. He died in 1944, shot down over Germany. Sergeant Pilot Arthur Banks was shot down over northern Italy in August 1944. He joined up with a local partisan group; was betrayed, captured and then shot by his Italian captors. He was awarded the George Cross posthumously.

Another aviator amongst former pupils was Sir Geoffrey de Havilland founder of the eponymous aircraft company, who served with distinction in the First World War.

In 1955 the Air Council, to commemorate the enormous contribution former pupils of St Edward's made to the war effort, presented the School with a stained glass window for the Chapel.

ST PETER'S SCHOOL, YORK

Ken Howard

The Great Hall

Founded by St Paulinus in 627 when he was Bishop of York, St Peter's is the third oldest school in Britain. In fact the writing of the Venerable Bede confirms the existence of a 'song school' at this time.

A song school and a grammar school were necessary concomitants for a new cathedral or abbey. The song school for the choristers and the grammar school for the teaching of Latin and more advanced types of education (church services were conducted in Latin.)

Two other saints were associated with the School in the 7th and 8th centuries: St Wilfred (Architect of the Synod of Whitby in 664) and St John of Beverley, both were Bishops of York and Masters of St Peter's School.

During the Middle Ages, St Peter's prospered because York was the base for campaigns against Scotland and its cathedral second only to Canterbury. In 1540, it suffered great hardship during The Reformation when Henry VIII seized the nearby St Mary's Abbey where the School's boarders lived. However in 1553, Henry's Catholic daughter Mary came to the throne and, to expiate her father's misdeeds, she re-endowed the School in 1557 and facilitated its move to more adequate premises in the Horsefair. This became a seminal moment, for it ensured that St Peter's would remain firmly Catholic. In fact successive Masters in the late 16th century were accused of being recusant. Guy Fawkes (1570-1606) became a pupil during this period and he converted to Catholicism despite having Protestant parents.

Against a background of religious persecution, Guy Fawkes, moved to Catholic Spain. He served with great distinction in the Spanish army in the Netherlands from 1593-1604. He returned to England in 1604 at the invitation of Robert Catesby in order to join his band of Catholic Conspirators. The Houses of Parliament were to be blown up, whilst in session, on 5th November 1605. Because of his knowledge of explosives, Guy Fawkes alone was to carry out the deed. However the Government received a tip-off and he was arrested. Catesby and the other conspirators had already fled but were apprehended and killed by government forces. No less than four of the thirteen principal conspirators were Peterites, the others being John and Christopher Wright , and Edward Oldcorne.

Guy Fawkes was executed in 1606 and every year on 5th November to celebrate the triumph of the Protestant faith over Catholicism bonfires and fireworks were lit with an effigy of the Pope being burnt. With the passing of time and to reflect the new mood of religious tolerance the effigy is now that of Guy Fawkes.

In course of the 18th century, St Peter's, like many other schools, went into decline but was rescued by an enlightened Master, Stephen Creyke (1827–1837) who transformed the School's fortunes. Shortly after this, a great opportunity presented itself when a school with new buildings on the edge of the city got into financial difficulties. The York Proprietory School sold its buildings to the Dean and Chapter who amalgamated the two schools.

The fine buildings which St Peter's acquired in 1844 are represented in Ken Howard's painting of The Great Hall which had been designed by the architect John Harper in 1838.

SEDBERGH SCHOOL

Dennis Roxby Bott

The Cloisters

In 1525 Roger Lupton, Provost of Eton founded a Chantry school in his native town of Sedbergh. Chantry Schools were much in evidence at this time being Catholic institutions, which in addition to teaching 'grammar' prayed for the souls of their founder. Most of them were dissolved between 1538 and 1549 by Henry VIII and his son Edward VI. Sedbergh was spared because of its link to St John's College, Cambridge, founded by Henry VIII's grandmother, Margaret Beaufort. In 1527 Lupton had established six scholarships to St John's College to be awarded exclusively to boys from the school and by its Deed of Foundation the College had the right to appoint its Headmaster. To this day, the School numbers a representative from St John's amongst its governors.

Arguably, there is no school in England with the environment and topography of Sedbergh. The grandeur of its setting amongst the mountains of what was once the West Riding of Yorkshire (the bureaucrats moved it into Cumbria in 1974) has helped shape its character and ethos. The Howgill Fells and more particularly, Winder Fell, form a magnificent backdrop to the school and provide a unique natural sporting facility.

Winters can be harsh in this part of the world and Sedbergh acquired a reputation as a tough school long before Gordonstoun made the Outward Bound approach a virtue. The epitome of this toughness is the famous 'Wilson Run', a ten mile cross country race over the Howgill Fells. It was instituted in 1881 by the Master whose name it bears and a time set in 1899 of 1 hour, 10 minutes and 16

seconds was the record for nearly one hundred years until it was dramatically broken by Charles Sykes in 1993 with a time of 1 hour, 8 minutes and 4 seconds.

Given its Spartan traditions, it is not surprising that Sedbergh has produced three England and one Scotland Rugby Union Captains: Wavell Wakefield; John Spencer; Will Carling and Mike Biggar. The England World Cup winning team of 2003 included another OS, Will Greenwood.

Sedbergh's traditional school motto *"Dura Virum Nutrix"* (a stern Nurse of Men) may in the past have seemed wholly inappropriate but since 2001, girls have been admitted to the School in ever increasing numbers. This was a deliberate move by the then Headmaster, Christopher Hirst, to give a better balance to the School. It rightly retains its formidable reputation on the sports field but away from that provides a happy and caring environment for all its pupils, regardless of ability and sports prowess.

Dennis Roxby Bott's painting of The Cloisters portrays the School in its unique setting beneath the Howgill Fells; part of the Yorkshire Dales National Park. The School is particularly proud of its cloisters, one of the few officially listed War Memorials to be located within a school. Every known name of an old boy or member of staff who died during the First and Second World Wars is recorded on its walls.

SHERBORNE SCHOOL

John Doyle

The Courts

Sherborne School was founded in 1550 under a Royal Charter granted by Edward VI, that most zealously Protestant of Tudor monarchs, who in his short life (he died at 16) founded or re-founded six schools and now has ten schools named after him.

However, Sherbourne's origins date back to the 8th century when a tradition of education was begun by St Aldhelm, Bishop of Sherbourne, whose Benedictine Abbey spawned a Latin school. In the 9th century King Alfred's biographer and Chaplain, Asser, was appointed to the See of Sherborne where it is thought Alfred received his early education. Asser is buried at Sherborne as are two of Alfred's older brothers, Ethelbald and Ethelbert, who were successive Kings of Wessex before Alfred.

The School exudes history, with the magnificent Abbey rising high above the school campus with its eclectic mix of ancient, medieval and renaissance architecture. The School's central core as represented by the Old School Room (1606) and School House (1670) were later augmented by older monastic buildings which were converted for school use. These include the present Library (formerly the 15th century Guesten Hall); Chapel (formerly the Abbots Hall) and Headmaster's rooms which include elements from the Anglo Saxon period as well as the 12th – 15th centuries. In 1879, Big School Room was added, designed by R.H. Carpenter and Benjamin Inglelow, and is situated in The Courts, the central hub of the School.

The School flourished during the 17th and 18th centuries but by the middle of the 19th century the School had declined, pupil numbers having dropped to only 40.

Fortunately in 1850, a saviour arrived in the shape of a new Headmaster, Dr Hugo Daniel Harper. His revolutionary plans were eagerly embraced by the Governors, particularly as the railway arrived at Sherborne in 1860. He re-launched the School on 'modern' lines with new buildings, more staff and extra subjects, including mathematics and history.

This appealed to the Victorian zeal for education and new boarders appeared from all over the country. By the time Harper retired in 1877 there were 248 boarders and sixteen staff and it is true to say that Sherborne became the great school it is today due to his ethos and energy.

Sherborne has always been the training ground of the great West Country families, and generations of Raleighs, Careys, Chichesters and Hawkins are to be found on its rolls. In more recent times, it has produced Vice Chancellors of both Oxford and Cambridge Universities respectively; Sir Colin Lucas and Michael McCrum CBE. Other distinguished alumni include actors Jeremy Irons and Jon Pertwee and the England Test batsman, David Sheppard, who went on to become Bishop of Liverpool. The novelist Alec Waugh (older brother of Evelyn) was another Shirburnian who somewhat controversially wrote *"The Loom of Youth"* an account of his school days at Sherborne written when he was only seventeen.

John Doyle, himself an old Shiburnian, has lovingly painted a favourite view of his "alma mater"

SHREWSBURY SCHOOL

Denis Ryan

Annual Regatta

Shrewsbury School dates from 1552, one of the many schools founded or re-founded during the short reign of Edward VI. Although he was the official Founder and provided some monies; it was Thomas Ashton Headmaster from 1561 – 1571 who, by his connections, obtained most of the School's endowments and produced its statutes and ordinances. By 1586, it was the biggest school in England with 800 pupils. Sir Philip Sidney, the poet, soldier and courtier was a pupil of Ashton's from 1564 - 1568.

The School was originally located on Castle Hill in the centre of Shrewsbury where it remained until 1882 when it moved to a new site across the River Severn in Kingsland. The original buildings are now used as the Shrewsbury Town Library.

Like many schools, Shrewsbury entered a period of decline in the mid-17th century after The English Civil War and pupil numbers had reduced to only twenty, when Samuel Butler was appointed Headmaster. A renowned classical scholar, he transformed the School's fortunes to such an extent that by 1868 it was rated as one of the seven Great Schools in the Public Schools Act. This success meant that by the latter part of the 19th century it had outgrown its original premises.

The School's new premises on the spacious Kingsland estate had originally been a Foundling Hospital and Workhouse. The buildings were skilfully adapted for school use by the architect Arthur Blomfield who also added a chapel. Its location on the banks of the River Severn has allowed the School to gain an enviable reputation for rowing. The winning of the Princess Elizabeth Challenge Cup at Henley Royal Regatta in 2007 made this the School's 14th Rowing Eights win at the Regatta since 1919 and an achievement not matched by any other school over the same period. Also more Salopians have won Oxbridge Blues in the Boat Race than men from any other school except Eton.

Former pupils are called 'Old Salopians' although 'Salop' refers more particularly to Shropshire as a whole rather than its principal town of Shrewsbury. Its origins go back to Norman times when the invaders found the Saxon pronunciation difficult so they substituted 'Salopsescira' hence Salop. 'Old Salopians' include Charles Darwin and Samuel Butler, the writer, who was the grandson of the 17th century Headmaster. However 'Old Salopians' of a more recent vintage made a tremendous impact in 1961 when they founded the satirical magazine "Private Eye". Richard Ingrams, Willy Rushton, Christopher Brooker and Paul Foot were all at Shrewsbury in the 1950s where they edited the school magazine "The Salopian" which was in effect the forerunner of "Private Eye". As if this were not enough drollery, a few years later in 1969, another Old Salopian, Michael Palin was a founder member of 'Monty Python's Flying Circus'. It was a Salopian, J.C. Thring, who was instrumental in drafting the original 1862 Rules of Association Football which effectively codified the non-handling branch of football; soccer, as distinct from rugby.

STOCKPORT GRAMMAR SCHOOL

Clifford Bayly

View from the Sports Field

Sir Edmund Shaa, the founder of Stockport Grammar School, was involved in one of the most controversial episodes in English History when as Mayor of London, in 1483, he officially offered the crown of England to the Duke of Gloucester, the notorious King Richard III. Born in the Mottram district of Stockport, to parents of modest means, he rose to fame and fortune in London before, by the terms of his Will, founding Stockport Grammar School in 1487.

In 1450 Edmund Shaa moved to London and was apprenticed to Robert Botiller, a goldsmith, and, according to the records of The Goldsmiths' Company, was allowed to practice his craft professionally in 1458. Success quickly followed. In 1462 Edward IV appointed him to the office of Engraver to the Tower Mint and all other Mints in England and Calais, and he became Mayor of London in 1482. He was clearly an astute politician, for having sided with Richard III, he also served Richard's usurper, Henry Tudor. Shaa was knighted during Richard's short reign and granted possession of a large estate in Essex by Henry VII.

Stockport Grammar School began life in the Davenport Chapel of St Mary's Parish Church in Stockport, administered from afar by The Goldsmiths' Company in London. Over the centuries the relationship between School and Company was to blow hot and cold and it was thanks to the generosity of a local benefactor, Alexander Lowe, that the School gained a permanent home in Chestergate in 1607 where it remained until 1832. Just prior to the end of this period, The Goldsmiths' Company seems to have reawakened interest in the School and arranged for the building of a new and more spacious school at Greek Street. The Goldsmiths' own architect, Philip Hardwick, designed the School in the Tudor Gothic style. However by the latter part of the 19th Century, relations with the Goldsmiths deteriorated to an all-time low and connections were finally severed in 1894.

In 1902, Stockport Grammar School came under the jurisdiction of the newly created Board of Education who, in the face of rising numbers, indicated that there was serious overcrowding and, furthermore, the School fell short of modern standards. There was no room to expand on the Greek Street site, so the only solution was to move. A new site was acquired next to the London and North Western Railway Station at Davenport, a mile from the town centre. London architects, Spalding & Theakston, were commissioned to draw up plans, even though the Board of Education thought the design of the School was over ornate and the cost £32,000 (£2.3million today) too high. The Governors then appealed to local Educational Charities. These responded magnificently: the Ephraim Hallam Charity alone providing £22,500. The School opened in January 1916 and proved to be an immediate success with pupil numbers rising from 150 to 250 by the end of the year.

In 1937, a banquet was held in the Hallam Hall to celebrate the 450th Anniversary of the School. The principal guest was the Prime Warden of The Worshipful Company of Goldsmiths whose presence marked the coming together again of The Company and its former school and they are to this day its official patrons.

SUTTON VALENCE SCHOOL

Dennis Flanders

Sutton Valence Village

Sutton Valence School was founded in 1576 by William Lambe, a native of the village. He went to London as an apprentice cloth maker and rose to become Master of The Clothworkers' Company and a Chorister at Henry VIII's Chapel Royal.

The School remained in the centre of the village for over three hundred years, catering mainly for the sons of clothworkers and local farming gentry. During this time it remained under the governance of The Clothworkers' Company and never had more than 100 pupils. However in 1910, things changed when the School was taken over by the United Westminster Schools' Foundation whose other schools are Emmanuel School and Westminster School, both in London. The new regime encouraged pupils from a wider geographical and social background. This required an expansion in the School's limited accommodation, and a new school was built on a site above the village donated by Mr W.E. Horne who was also a Master of The Clothworkers' Company. The new School's site covers over 100 acres and today's roll stands at over 500 pupils.

The School is situated on top of the Chart Hills, a sandstone ridge overlooking the Weald of Kent. The view from the School over the Weald is quite breathtaking. The Chart Hills are part of the Greensand Ridge which runs through Kent, Surrey, Hampshire and Sussex to the south and parallel to the North Downs. Its crowning glory is Leith Hill which rises to 997ft (The highest point in Southern England).

Nearby is the 12th century Sutton Valence Castle, once the home of William de Valence, Earl of Pembroke (1225 – 1296) after whom the village is named; a half-brother of Henry III. On a hill facing the castle is BM (Bloody Mountain) where alledgedly a terrible and bloody battle was fought between the invading Romans and the Ancient Britons. It is now part of the School's playing fields!

The timeless picture opposite of a tranquil village with its varied roof lines contains many elements associated with the School. The old 19th century school building can be seen on the right at the end of the High Street. Adjacent are the 16th century William Lambe Almshouses, now turned to school use. The new School can be seen looming over the village in the top right hand corner. Dennis started this painting on a glorious Saturday in February, 1993, seated on the steps of an old chapel which is now used as an art department of the School. He spied some school hockey players and was keen to incorporate them into the picture, resplendent in their yellow and black school colours. It turned out, however, that they were the opposition and he subsequently changed the colour of their strip to blue; the Sutton Valence colours.

Among famous Old Suttonians are the athlete Sidney Wooderson, who held the World Mile record between 1937-1942 and after whom the School's sports hall is named; Sir Charles Groves, the Orchestral Conductor and Terence Cuneo, the railway poster artist.

TAUNTON SCHOOL

Hubert Pragnell

School House

Victorian England was a time of great religious fervour. Religion was central to daily life and seen as the promoter of the Nation's social and moral needs. It was also a time of great denominational rivalry between the established church (Church of England) and the Independents or Congregationalists including the Baptists. Church building by all denominations, including the Roman Catholics and Methodists, showed a marked increase.

However, it was the political privilege retained by the Church of England in certain significant areas, notably education, that so irked the other denominations. The Factory Bill of 1843 which proposed that the teachers and managers of schools for factory children should be members of the Established Church, provoked such vociferous opposition from dissenting denominations that it had to be abandoned. The Universities of Oxford and Cambridge were closed to those who were not members of the Established Church, and it was not until the passing of the University Tests Act of 1871 that all religious barriers were finally removed at the Universities.

The Independents formed themselves into the Independent Denomination of Protestant Dissenters, who in principal were opposed to the structures and practices of the Established Church of England. They were, in essence, Puritans who regarded the reformation of the church under Elizabeth I as incomplete as it still permitted what they regarded as undesirable practices and ceremonies.

It was against this background that Taunton School was founded in 1847 as the formidable sounding 'West of England Dissenters' Proprietary School'. The curriculum was to include not only the study of the Bible but also Greek, Hebrew and Church history. The day began and ended with religious observance, with Chapel services being attended twice on Sundays.

The School's first site was at the southern end of town, and pupils attended services at the Presbyterian Church (now United Reformed) in Paul Street and the Congregational Chapel in North Street. The Ministers of these churches were joint secretaries of the School.

In 1870 the School's Governors purchased a site at the northern end of Taunton on Staplegrove Road. They commissioned the architect Joseph James to build a Gothic structure using grey limestone from the Mendip Hills. The façade is dominated by a 50 foot tower and this building still dominates the School's 90 acre campus today and is a grade II listed building.

The School did not acquire its own chapel until 1907. It was the gift of Lord Winterstoke (Henry Wills) who was a director of the Bristol based family firm of Wills Tobacco. The architect was his cousin Sir Frank Wills. The Chapel was built using Guiting Oolitic limestone from Gloucestershire. The golden honey colour of this Cotswold limestone is a pleasing contrast to the grey of the main building.

Today Taunton is an interdenominational school and in 1976 merged with the nearby Weirfield Girls' School to become one of the earliest fully co-educational schools in England.

TONBRIDGE SCHOOL

Hubert Pragnell

Cricket on the Head.

The London Livery Companies have, since the 15th century, been involved in the administration and endowment of schools, in many cases as an adjunct to the foundation of almshouses. A case in point is The Skinners' Company, whose Master, Sir Andrew Judde, founded Tonbridge School in 1553 in his native town. On his death in 1558, his Will had provided for The Skinners' Company to become sole Trustees and Governors of the School, a function they exercise to this day. He also bequeathed to the School land in Gracechurch Street, in the City of London, and St Pancras, part of which was sold to the Midland Railway Company, which still brings in very good rental revenues.

The Skinners' Company is one of the Great Twelve Livery Companies out of a total of 84 flourishing in the City of London. They owe their origins to the trades which their Guilds administered and regulated in medieval England and whose names they bear. Their Order of Precedence has been hotly disputed for many years, leading to violence in the streets and even death. The Skinners and Merchant Taylors disputed sixth place and often fought for supremacy. Then, in 1484, The Lord Mayor of London, Thomas Billesdon, decreed that they should alternate on a yearly basis. This is said to be the origin of the expression 'all at sixes and sevens'.

Tonbridge School, thanks to Judde's substantial endowments, and the generosity of The Skinners' Company, survived the national malaise afflicting education in the 17th and 18th centuries. In 1774 pupil numbers dropped to only seventeen.

In the mid-19th century, numbers rose to around 200 to satisfy the appetite of newly emerging Victorian middle classes for educational provision for their sons.

In 1890 a remarkable Headmaster was appointed, Revd Joseph Wood, a product of Manchester Grammar School and Balliol College, Oxford. Such was his reputation and energy that, in the eight years of his stewardship, pupil numbers rose from 175 to 447. Wood virtually rebuilt the School adding a new science building, an impressive clock tower and a spacious hall (Big School). Wood even overcame the objections of the Charity Commission's constant refusal to countenance the building of a new chapel. Consecrated in 1902, it dominated the School scene, not only in size but in appearance because it was built predominantly of red brick of different shades and faced with stone. In many ways it is not dissimilar to Keble College Oxford which had also attracted controversy.

No treatise on Tonbridge School would be complete without mention of 'The Head' – the lovely 1st XI cricket ground regarded as one of the best pitches in the country. The field on which it is situated was purchased in 1826 and levelled using earth and labour from the new railway workings. The vista looking across The Head towards the main School is surreal and is a favourite subject for artists. It has also produced two England Cricket Captains, Colin Cowdrey (1959 – 1969) and his son Chris (1988). Fittingly, Colin became Master of The Skinners' Company in 1986.

UPPINGHAM SCHOOL

Dennis Roxby Bott

Chapel and School House Quad

Uppingham, with a population of less than 4000, is a small and attractive old market town in the unspoilt countryside of Rutland. According to Arthur Mee in his 1937 edition *"The Kings England"* "its chief industry is the making of fine Englishmen and exporting them to the four corners of the world". And in Uppingham "it has one of England's finest schools with a reputation far beyond the borders of our land".

It is not often that two schools within 20 miles of each other are simultaneously founded by the same benefactor. The benefactor was Archdeacon Robert Johnson, a local rector, who in 1584, a few years before the Spanish Armada, founded both Uppingham and Oakham Schools within England's smallest county of Rutland. For nearly 300 years Uppingham School was housed in an Elizabethan Schoolroom behind the Church and Market Square (still in use today). During this time it remained a small and unremarkable grammar school.

However, in 1853, Edward Thring became Headmaster and in 12 years numbers increased from 43 to 300. Such expansion required a significant programme of school building with the addition of a new schoolroom and chapel designed by the architect, George Edmund Street, who had designed the Law Courts in The Strand, London. There rapidly followed boarding houses, a laboratory, a museum and a gymnasium. (one of the first to be installed in a school). All this building work was accomplished using the local ironstone which gives the school buildings a wonderful homogenous quality.

Edward Thring was educated at Eton and King's College, Cambridge where he

was elected a Fellow. His first priority on becoming Headmaster was to change the whole ethos of education.

After his experience at Eton where conditions were notoriously tough, he resolved that life at his school should have comfort, leisure and happiness. The boys instead of being herded together, were each given a study. He also introduced non academic activities such as music, arts and crafts as well as organised games, although classics still held pride of place in the curriculum. He was keen to develop character as well as intellect.

He was truly a man of action which was demonstrated when in 1876 disaster struck. Five boys died of typhoid as a result of the town's primitive sewerage system causing parents to withdraw their children from the school. To avoid possible ruin, Thring evacuated the whole school to a healthier location. The Civic Authorities in Uppingham, facing an economic depression as a result of the move, installed a new sewerage system and a triumphant Edward Thring brought the school back to Uppingham in time for the 1887 Summer Term. This all attracted much favourable publicity in the national press and the event is still remembered in an annual Chapel service.

Edward Thring died in harness in 1887 having served as Headmaster at Uppingham for 34 years, during which time he made it one of the best Independent Schools in Britain. He wrote many books on educational subjects including his magnus opus *"The Theory and Practice of Teaching"*. In 1869 he also founded The Headmasters' Conference. He was probably the greatest of the Victorian educationalists, a worthy successor to Rugby's Thomas Arnold.

WELLINGTON COLLEGE

Dennis Flanders

The South Front

The view opposite from the Master's Lodge contains Wellington's two distinct architectural styles: the initial classical Jacobean for the main body of the College, on the left, and the later Gothic Chapel to the right. It sets the tone for this magnificent school, which occupies four hundred acres of parkland amidst the pinewoods, heather and rhododendrons of East Berkshire.

Wellington College was founded in 1853 by public subscription, as a memorial to Arthur Wellesley, First Duke of Wellington, who had died a year earlier. He was a great soldier, statesman, victor at Waterloo and twice Prime Minister of Great Britain, in 1830 and 1834.

The idea of a school was born at Balmoral during a meeting of Queen Victoria, Prince Albert and the Prime Minister of the day, Lord Derby. It was intended that the College would be for the education of the orphans of army officers. Its location has little to do with the proximity to Sandhurst Military College, but more to do with the generosity of a local resident, Mr Robert Gibson, who donated 12 acres of land.

The architect chosen for the school was John Shaw Jnr, whose designs were heavily influenced by the work of Christopher Wren, two centuries earlier. His work was much admired by Prince Albert, because of its classical Jacobean style as opposed to the more common Gothic, popular at the time. He was at this time architect to Eton College.

The College is built of red brick with stone string courses and dressings, mansard roofs and oval dormer windows. When the College opened in 1859, the chapel had not yet been built. Its first Master, Edward Benson, wanted it built in 19th century Gothic style and the ubiquitous George Gilbert Scott was chosen as

architect. One can only marvel at the forbearance of Shaw and Prince Albert in yielding to the Master's desire for a Gothic chapel. With such powers of persuasion it was hardly surprising that Edward Benson eventually became Archbishop of Canterbury.

As well as admitting orphans of army officers, help was given to serving officers to send their sons to Wellington. As a result, a very large number of distinguished army officers are Old Wellingtonians and during the course of two World Wars, 15 received the Victoria Cross. In 1952 a Supplementary Royal Charter extended admission to the orphans of deceased officers of the Royal Navy, Royal Marines and Royal Air Force. Today, however, only a minority of the children at the school are the sons and daughters of military officers.

Music, drama, the arts and sport are all part of the eclectic mix of everyday life at Wellington. Ten or twelve musical and theatrical productions are performed in the College's modern and well equipped theatre every year. The College has a national reputation for prowess in games and it is an interesting fact that Wellington and Marlborough were the first Independent Schools to compete at rugby. In fact, in 1871, Wellington College was one of the 21 founding members of The Rugby Football Union at its inaugural meeting in the Pall Mall Restaurant in London. Blackheath and Harlequins were also present although surprisingly Rugby School was not.

Today Wellington is one of the great national boarding schools and in 2006 became fully co-educational. It retains, however, its eponymous link with the Iron Duke, proudly displaying, in a glass case, the cloak, helmet and sword Wellington wore at Waterloo.

WESTMINSTER SCHOOL

Dennis Flanders

Little Dean's Yard.

In the latter part of the 19th century schools based in the centre of London started to move out to more spacious locations in the Home Counties. When the Dean and Chapter of Westminster School proposed a similar move there was such an uproar of dissent from pupils and old boys that the plan was abandoned. After nearly 900 years of existence at Westminster at the heart of the Church and Government, a move to less prestigious surroundings was unthinkable.

In 1179 Pope Alexander III made the maintenance of schools obligatory for all cathedral and monastic establishments, including Westminster, which at this was a Benedictine monastery. In 1540 when Henry VIII dissolved Westminster Abbey, along with other monasteries in England, he ensured Westminster School's continuance by endowing 40 King's Scholars and giving a Charter to that effect.

Elizabeth I re-founded the School in 1560 providing new statutes which provided for the selection of 40 Queen's Scholars. However legal separation from the Abbey was not achieved until implementation of the Public Schools Act of 1868.

The School buildings, approached through the archway of Dean's Yard are all within the precincts of Westminster Abbey, and in parts older than the Abbey itself, particularly 'School' originally a monastic dormitory, dating back to 1090. It is still the School's main hall.

One of Westminster's most illustrious Head Masters was Dr Richard Busby who reigned from 1638-1695. Despite openly supporting Charles I during The English Civil War he survived The Commonwealth; The Restoration; and attended Oliver Cromwell's funeral. He even had to deal with the vicissitudes of The Plague and The Great Fire of London. At the end of his term he had made the School so prosperous that it was considered equal to Eton and Winchester.

Like many London based Public Schools, Westminster helped develop Association Football into the game we know today (as distinct from the handling game developed at Rugby). Forward passing and the offside rule can be attributed to Westminster and Charterhouse and were adopted by the Football Association in 1867.

However a game unique to Westminster is 'The Greaze' which has been held 'up school' (in the School Hall) every Shrove Tuesday since 1753. It involves the head cook ceremoniously tossing a horsehair reinforced pancake over a high bar which, until the 16th century, curtained off the Lower School. Members of the School fight for the pancake watched by the Dean of Westminster Abbey (who is Chairman of Governors), the Headmaster and the entire School. The boy who secures the largest piece of pancake is awarded a gold sovereign which he gives back in return for the Dean calling "a play" (a day's holiday).

WHITGIFT SCHOOL, CROYDON

Dennis Flanders

Andrew Quadrangle

The School was founded in 1596 by John Whitgift, Archbishop of Canterbury, in the centre of Croydon. His eponymous legacy, 'The Whitgift Foundation' today includes two other Independent Schools in the Croydon area: Old Palace School and Trinity School. The Foundation provides bursaries and scholarships to those families unable to afford the full tuition fees. Additionally, sheltered accommodation and nursing care are provided through the Whitgift Almshouses (officially known as 'The Hospital of Holy Trinity'). Today the Foundation has a large and valuable property portfolio in Croydon, including the freehold of Cobham Hurst golf course and the freehold and significant rental income from the Whitgift Centre, one of the busiest shopping centres in South East England.

In 1931, Whitgift School moved to its present forty five acre parkland setting at Haling Park, South Croydon. In the 16th century Haling Park was the home of Lord Howard of Effingham who commanded the English fleet against the Spanish Armada. The original site was retained by the Whitgift Foundation and became the home of Trinity School until 1965 when it moved nearby to make way for the Whitgift Shopping Centre.

The School, which caters for 1200 Day Boys, has in the past twenty years added two facilities which are the envy of most other schools in their scope and scale. In 1990 one of the largest and most innovative educational building projects in Britain was completed to provide an integral facility for science, technology, art and design together with a library and resource centre of exceptional quality.

In 2002 a multi-million pound sports complex was completed, which is fitting as Whitgift has played host to several 1st Class and One Day games played by Surrey Cricket Club.

An unusual feature for a school located in suburbia is its interest in wildlife. In 2005, the world famous naturalist David Attenborough visited the School to open its artificially created lakes around which wildlife abounds. There are enclosures for the endangered red squirrels, albinos and wallabies (a gift from the Queen), in addition to the peacocks which were originally presented to the School in 1936.

As with a lot of schools, Whitgift has its own 'Mr Kipps' character in the shape of Mr F.H.G. Percy whose connection with the School spanned eighty years. He became a pupil in central Croydon from 1922 until 1930 when he went to university. He returned in 1936 to the new school in South Croydon to teach until 1976 when he retired and became the School's Archivist; a post he held until 2002. He died in 2006 at the age of 96. His memory lives on through the F.H.G. Percy Essay Prize which his family instituted after his death.

The painting opposite is of the Andrew Quadrangle, a peaceful and majestic setting containing a beautiful Oriel window on the library building to the left of the picture. The Quadrangle takes its name from S.O. Andrew who was Headmaster of the school 1903–1927. Also in the painting are two of the legendary peacocks.

135

WINCHESTER COLLEGE
Dennis Flanders

Chamber Court

Winchester College, one of the oldest Schools in England, owes its foundation in 1382 to William of Wykeham, (c. 1324 - 1404), Bishop of Winchester. He was born at Wickham in Hampshire and became a truly gifted prelate and statesman and one of the most powerful men in 14th century England. Having served Edward III as Surveyor of Windsor Castle and other royal castles from 1356-1359 he was appointed Keeper of the Privy Seal and Secretary to the King in 1364. In 1367 he was appointed Bishop of Winchester and Chancellor of England (equivalent to our modern day Prime Minister). This latter post he held until 1371 and again, under Edward's successor Richard II, from 1389-91.

William of Wykeham was a management man, a corporate planner on a grand scale. He had first founded New College Oxford in 1379 to fill the shortage in the secular clergy (who provided the nation's civil service) caused by The Black Death. Winchester was founded to educate seventy poor scholars who would then proceed to his Oxford foundation. Additionally, there was provision for ten Fellows and sixteen choirboys (called Quiristers) and up to ten fee paying pupils known as 'Commoners'. The Commoners soon exceeded ten and while seventy Scholars continue to this day to receive bursaries in accordance with the Founder's intention, over the centuries Commoners came to outnumber them by a multiple of ten.

Probably no school has had a greater influence on English education than Winchester. It has for many centuries served as a model for other boarding schools and William of Wykeham has been called 'the father of the Public School system'. King Henry VI visited Winchester three times and laid the foundation stone of Eton on earth he had brought up to Windsor from Chamber Court at Winchester. Eton's first Provost, William Waynfleet, (1395-1486) came from

Winchester, as did Thomas Arnold of Rugby, in the 19th century. Alumni of Winchester are known as Wykehamists, after their founder, and it invests them with a certain intellectual confidence.

Winchester College is famous for its wonderful medieval buildings designed by Master Mason, William de Wynford, though Wykeham would have had a significant input being a very talented architect himself. It is the oldest continuously inhabited school in Britain. The heart of the College is Chamber Court, shown in the painting opposite, which housed the original seventy poor Scholars and was from the beginning the centre of college life. Also seen in the painting is the Chapel Tower and to the right, the Hall. The 14th century Gothic chapel has one of the earliest examples of a wooden lierne-vaulted roof.

Over the centuries, various eminent architects have contributed to the College's development. The 17th century school room known as 'School' has been attributed (without authority) to Sir Christopher Wren. Moberly Court and Flint Court were designed by William Butterfield in the late 19th century not long after his masterpiece, Keble College Oxford. Butterfield was also responsible for rebuilding the Chapel Tower in 1863.

In 1898 Basil Champneys completed the Queen Anne style Old Museum which was reminiscent of his earlier work at Newnham College, Cambridge. Sir Herbert Baker was, in 1924, responsible for the War Cloister. The former Headmaster's House (now the Library and offices) by G.S. Repton, was completed in 1842 and can be seen along with all of the other architectural gems, by means of one of the many daily guided tours.

137

WOLVERHAMPTON GRAMMAR SCHOOL

Jane Carpanini

Main Building

In 1509, the year of Henry VIII's coronation, the Lord Mayor of London, was Sir Stephen Jenyns, a native of Wolverhampton and Master of The Guild of Merchant Taylors. He was one of the wealthiest men in England and in 1519 reputedly paid more tax than any other citizen. He was born in 1448 and it was the accepted practice for men of good fortune to provide for their home towns either almshouses or schools or even both. In 1512 Sir Stephen Jenyns founded a grammar school and gave to the Merchant Taylors the Manor of Rushock (near Kidderminster) in order that they might direct its income to the maintenance of his school.

A site for the school was found in St John's Street near to the town centre. Here the School resided for 363 years until the area became heavily polluted by industry and conditions in the school were cramped and the buildings dilapidated.

In 1875 the School moved to its present location on Compton Road, a twenty three acre site only a mile from the town centre. The move was financed by mortgaging the Rushock Estate selling the old school and a very successful public subscription. A further subscription in 1897 enabled the School to open a science building, a great innovation at the time, but the School found that it was still short of classrooms.

The Education Act of 1902 led to the creation of Local Education Authorities with the power to make grants to Independent Schools. In 1907, in return for a grant of £300 from Wolverhampton Local Education Authority, the School accepted 25 elementary pupils free of charge. Thus Wolverhampton Grammar

School became a Direct Grant school and was thereby able to finance the expansion and pupil numbers rose from 160 in 1907 to 560 in 1923. The School received an annual direct grant until after the Second World War.

After the Education Act 1944 the rules changed and it became clear that the School could no longer afford to remain independent. In 1949 it accepted Voluntary Aided Status which abolished fees and gave Wolverhampton Local Education Authority effective control, although the Trustees were still responsible for any capital expenditure such as new school buildings.

By the middle of the 1970s, plans were being made to include the School in Wolverhampton's Comprehensive System which came to a head in 1977 with the decision of the Local Education Authority to cease sending boys to the school. Accepting that there was no option but a return to Independent status, a fund raising appeal was launched which raised £700,000, the most successful campaign ever run by any school up till that time. In 1979 a fee paying First Year joined the School and in 1980 the new Conservative Government introduced the Assisted Places Scheme. Wolverhampton Grammar School became the largest user of Assisted Places Funding in England with over 47% of its pupils aided in this way.

The abolition of the Assisted Places Scheme by the incoming Labour Government in 1997 returned the School to complete independence. By then the School was fully co-educational having admitted girls into the Sixth Form in 1984 and into the First Form in 1992.

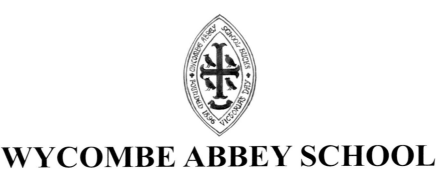

WYCOMBE ABBEY SCHOOL

Jane Carpanini

Main School Building

Wycombe Abbey School was founded in 1896 by Jane Frances Dove. Born in 1847 she was the eldest of eight children.

The Dove family had numbered a Bishop of Peterborough amongst their ancestors so it was not surprising that Jane Frances Dove's father, The Revd John Thomas Dove, took up a curacy in London at Christ Church, Marylebone. It was during this time that Jane Frances Dove attended Queen's College, Harley Street; a pioneer in the quest for the higher education of girls. It was founded, in 1848, by Professor Frederick Mauric, a champion of women's education. Two other girls' schools followed; North London Collegiate (1850) and Cheltenham Ladies' College (1854).

Coincidentally to the founding of schools for girls, colleges for ladies were being founded in Oxford and Cambridge and it was to one of these, Girton, that Jane Frances Dove arrived towards the end of the Hitchin period in 1871. The move to new buildings just outside Cambridge took place in 1873 and Jane Frances Dove claimed to be the first student to cross the threshold. She was one of the first women to sit for the natural Sciences Tripos at Cambridge and in 1875 she secured the equivalent of a B.A., 'a Girton Certificate' (women were not awarded degrees at Cambridge until 1924).

Jane Frances Dove taught for a while at Cheltenham Ladies College. In 1877 she joined the staff of the recently founded girls' school, St Leonards School, St Andrews in Scotland where, in 1882, she became Headmistress, due to the ill health of the incumbent Miss Lumsden. After 13 years of great success at St Leonards, 'Miss Dove', as she was now styled, resigned in order that she might found her own girls' school in England.

After looking at a great number of properties she finally found her ideal: Lord Carrington's house, Wycombe Abbey, in Buckinghamshire, which was purchased for £20,000 including thirty acres of land. It was delightfully situated in the Chiltern Hills, 36 miles from London on the outskirts of what was then a charming old country town, High Wycombe. The School officially opened on 26th September 1896.

Prior to 1798, Wycombe Abbey had been a large medieval manor house known as 'Loakes Manor' which in the 18th century was owned by Lord Shelburne , British Prime Minister (1792-3). In 1798, Loakes Manor was purchased by Lord Carrington who engaged the leading architect of the day, Sir Thomas Wyatt. He transformed the Jacobean mansion into a Gothic masterpiece reminiscent of Wyatt's Gothic extravaganza, Fonthill Abbey, in Wiltshire. His other works include the Radcliffe Observatory in Oxford; Liverpool Town Hall and college buildings in Oxford at Christchurch, Oriel and St Peter's.

Miss Dove retired as Headmistress in 1910 and was honoured with the title of 'Dame Frances Dove' in 1928. She died in 1942, six days before her 95th birthday.

Daws Hill was purchased in 1928, by a later Headmistress, Miss Winifred Maitland Crosthwaite, bringing the School site up to 150 acres.

INDEX OF PEOPLE

INDEX OF PEOPLE

INDEX OF PEOPLE